From a Polish Country House Kitchen

From a Polish Country House Kitchen

90 RECIPES FOR THE
ULTIMATE COMFORT FOOD

Anne Applebaum & Danielle Crittenden
Photographs by **Bogdan & Dorota Biały**

CHRONICLE BOOKS
SAN FRANCISCO

Library of Congress Cataloging-in-Publication Data available.
ISBN 978-1-4521-1055-4

Manufactured in China

Designed by Alice Chau
Typesetting by Alice Chau & Helen Lee
Photographs by Bogdan Biały
Additional styling by Dorota Biały

Some of the recipes in this book include raw eggs, meat, poultry,
seafood, or shellfish. Consumed raw, these foods pose a risk
for bacteria that are killed by proper cooking and should not
be consumed by pregnant women, infants, small children, the
elderly, or people with autoimmune conditions. Please purchase
from trusted sources and read and follow recipe instructions
carefully. The authors and Chronicle Books disclaim any and all
liability for injuries suffered while consuming any of the raw
foods described in this book.

10 9 8 7 6 5 4

Chronicle Books LLC
680 Second Street
San Francisco, California 94107
www.chroniclebooks.com

Contents

Preface
page 25

Introduction
page 30

Chapter One / Appetizers and Starters
page 40

Chapter Two / Soups
page 58

Chapter Three / Salads and Vegetables
page 94

Chapter Four / Main Courses
page 128

Chapter Five / Pierogi and Pancakes
page 198

Chapter Six / Desserts
page 226

Chapter Seven / From a Polish Larder
page 258

Index
page 280

Preface

Anne and I are unlikely cookbook writers. She is an acclaimed, prize-winning historian and columnist who has spent most of her career covering the politics of Eastern Europe and Russia. I'm a Washington-based journalist, editor, and author who has mostly occupied herself with politics and women's issues. And many people would suggest that Polish food is an unlikely topic for a cookbook. We encountered this reaction throughout the writing of our book:

"What are you working on now?"

"A Polish cookbook."

Snickers or a perplexed look. Then, unfailingly, a reply along the following lines:

"How many recipes can you get out of boiled potatoes?"

Unfortunately for many of us, including the millions of North Americans with Polish ancestry, the very term "Polish cooking" conjures up memories of heavy, greasy dishes: the food of exile and poverty. And as Anne notes in her introduction, the reputation of Polish cooking was not enhanced by forty-five years of communism. But what you'll find in the following pages is not, as one might say, your grandmother's cooking.

Anne and I conceived this book a few summers ago on the back porch of her beautiful Polish country house, Dwor Chobielin. (*Dwor* means "manor.") Anne and her husband, Radek Sikorski (at that time Poland's defense minister), had invited a group of their American friends to come stay with them. Few of us had ever been to Poland, and none of us had yet visited the house that Anne and Radek had purchased for next to nothing right after communism fell in 1989. The couple had devoted two decades to rebuilding the ruined nineteenth-century pile near Bydgoszcz, quite literally from the ground up.

Radek and Anne led us on a leisurely bike ride through tall forests and winding side roads. We ate a picnic in the shadow of a lovely restored church. We stopped for ice cream in the main square of the nearby village of Nakło. Later, in lazy repose on their pillared back porch, wine glasses in hand, we admired the sweeping clipped lawn, which was bordered by rows of fruit trees. An impressive vegetable garden, with greenhouse, had been laid out near their picturesque old barn. Anne stepped out with a basket to collect the lush plums and soft lettuces that would later reappear at dinner.

At that moment we all had to concede that our preconceived notions of everything we'd see and eat in Poland were utterly and completely shattered. Our group had arrived in Warsaw a few days previously, and we'd taken some time to tour the magically rebuilt old city and other historical sites. Then we'd driven three hours to Chobielin, pausing to stop for lunch in the spectacular medieval village of Toruń (birthplace of Copernicus). The culinary renaissance we encountered everywhere thrillingly symbolized—as much as the new highways or glittering glass skyscrapers—Poland's national rebirth. The pierogi, or potato dumplings, that you can buy from supermarket freezers in North America, in no way resembled the delicate dumplings we were served in even the most modest of restaurant kitchens. These pierogi weren't doughy or oily or overstuffed with bland cheese. As delicate and translucent as Hong Kong's finest dim sum, they contained all sorts of original fillings. (My favorites were the ones that burst with the intensity of freshly picked wild mushrooms with an ever so slightly sour hint of sauerkraut.)

Beet soup—or what we so often associate with dishwatery thin and flavorless borscht—arrived as pink and silky as a sunset, occasionally with the exotic surprise of a bright yellow quail's egg yolk sinking into light streaks of sour cream. And then there was our introduction to game, meats that some lucky rural Poles—those who hunt or have friends who hunt—keep in their freezers the same way North Americans keep chicken, beef, and pork. For us, they opened up a whole new palate.

On this trip, too, Anne and I discovered that we shared a passion for cooking—and especially cooking for company. Given the political circles we both travel in, there are lots of occasions for it. I think neither of us can imagine a more pleasurable evening than sitting down to dinner with a mix of fascinating guests, whose lively conversation is fueled by home-cooked food that is hearty, unpretentious, and, above all, delicious.

Anne and I also discovered that we both shared a love of cooking with fresh, seasonal ingredients. At Chobielin and across Poland there still exists a culture that has all but vanished in the rich, sterile produce aisles of Western supermarkets, one that is only slowly being rediscovered in the growing prevalence of local farmers' markets. I noticed that even the most urbanized Poles still knew how to string and dry mushrooms, pickle cucumbers, and make jam. These skills may have been enforced by decades of economic hardship, as Anne describes in her introduction, but they deliver pure joy: Even a poor Polish farmer who pulls his own potato from the ground will experience something far tastier than the wealthy Western European who plucks his potato from the mass-produced selections stacked in pyramids at his grocery store. Anyone who has ever grown something as simple as a cherry tomato on her city patio knows that her sweet and juicy little crop in no way resembles the waxy red marbles the supermarkets sell in January. A carrot pulled fresh from the dirt, a young sugary beet with its crisp veined leaves, a velvety green bean picked right off its vine—these are what we tasted from Anne's own garden, and they tasted like nothing I'd had before. Her example inspired me to seek out such freshness when I returned back home to DC; since then I've been growing small crops of lettuces in my backyard, and enjoying the seasonal produce that has become increasingly more available from nearby Virginia and Maryland farms.

It's in that spirit that Anne and I present this cookbook: the food of a high culture, now reborn; the food of so many of our ancestors, reinterpreted for health-conscious contemporaries. Months after our magical summer visit to Chobielin, and a century after my husband's Eastern European ancestors stumbled off a boat at Ellis Island, I found myself trying, as they did in their Bronx apartments, to re-create the cuisine of a homeland that still calls to us. I looked forward to receiving every new recipe-packed e-mail from Anne, painstakingly translated so that I might be able to follow them (not always successfully, e.g., "Is a shot glass of vodka the same as an ounce of vodka, or are your shot glasses bigger than ours?"). I sought out local sources for venison and wild boar—not as difficult as I'd imagined. My neighborhood butcher carries both. I've noticed that game generally, including the deliciously beefy elk or our native buffalo, is becoming more common both in specialty and farmers' markets.

Anne and I then cooked and tested these dishes an ocean apart from each other, Anne in her Polish country kitchen, I in my urban American one. I'm sure that our dishes tasted different, even though born from the same recipes. The very nature of her soil, of the way her chickens and cows came to market, would produce an accent in her dishes that differed as distinctly as a regional accent in a voice.

But no matter: Good, simple food is good, simple food. We hope you will agree.

—Danielle Crittenden

Introduction

"Commies love concrete," wrote P. J. O'Rourke in his classic account of a visit to Poland in the drab 1980s. "Everything is made of it: streets, buildings, floors, walls, ceilings, roofs, window frames, lamp posts, statues, benches, plus some of the food, I think."

It was an enduring image, both of Polish architecture and of Polish cuisine, in America and Europe. It was not an entirely unfair image, either. Before 1989, Poland was a country of strikes, electricity cuts, and shortages. Polish grocery stores contained salt, canned fish, vinegar, and not much else. In Polish restaurants, sullen waiters handed their customers long menus, invariably featuring dishes that were not available.

Of course if you knew where to go and what to ask for, there were culinary surprises. Even in the darkest days of martial law, the Hotel Europejski, in Warsaw, served an excellent steak tartare. Some of the city's milk bars sold delicious pierogi filled with sweet cheese. Excellent fresh vegetables could be found at the farmers' markets that had sprung up, despite restrictions upon private enterprise, in most major cities. Through connections—in Warsaw there was a "veal lady" who went from house to house—one could get excellent meat and cheeses as well. Almost everyone had an aunt or grandmother in the country who made jam and pickles. For a brief period in the late 1980s and early 1990s, just as communism was collapsing and the free market was taking over, a jar of black Beluga caviar that would empty a wallet in London or Paris could be purchased in Warsaw's Polna market for a handful of change.

In the years that followed, Polish cuisine, which had been something of a national secret—sometimes restaurants were hidden away in private houses along with the underground printing presses—burst into the open, along with free trade unions and democratic political parties. The first phase was chaotic, and often derivative. In Warsaw, new restaurants served pretentious French food, together with overpriced French wine. Meanwhile, Polish versions of "pizza"—melted cheese and sautéed mushrooms on sourdough bread—appeared in the provinces, along with McDonald's and even cheaper imitations.

But in recent years, Polish cooks, both amateur and professional, have returned to their roots, launching a revival of Polish cooking on a national scale. The most fashionable Warsaw and Krakow restaurants no longer serve foreign food with fancy names. They serve *szmalec*, an old-fashioned peasant spread made of pork fat, instead of butter. They offer black bread to spread it on, instead of baguettes. They make robust pork and duck dishes instead of grilled tuna and wasabi, although, I hasten to add, grilled tuna and wasabi are available in Warsaw as well.

Creative chefs have also begun to experiment with, and promote the use of, Polish ingredients. The entrepreneurial Gessler family began opening restaurants specializing in new versions of traditional dishes, from herring tartare to exotic pierogi. The prolific Magda Gessler has produced a clutch of cookbooks that fuse Polish and foreign cuisines, as well as a television program, *Kitchen Revolution*, that does the same. Another member of the family, Marta Gessler, has a newspaper column that promotes quirky versions of traditional dishes, from strawberry soup to meringue desserts (a version of which we include here).

The Slow Food movement has also taken off in Poland, and has spread to restaurants such as Bulaj in the resort town of Sopot, which specializes in local fish and local game, served with locally grown organic vegetables. Slow Food entrepreneurs have also begun to raise the quality of many traditional foods, from sheep's milk cheese, a traditional product of Poland's mountainous south, to mead (fermented honey), which now comes in dozens of variations.

The cuisine has been modernized, and is less fatty and less salty than it used to be. Previously scarce vegetables now play a leading role. But the new cuisine is recognizably Polish, not pseudo-French or mock-Italian, and is much the better for it. Outside the major cities, provincial restaurants—*karczmy*—now serve soup and pickles instead of hamburgers.

What is true in restaurants is equally true in homes. In fact, my own acquaintance with Polish food doesn't really come from restaurants at all. Although I do appreciate some of the new ones, I learned to cook with Polish ingredients because I often didn't have anything else.

In 1988, my husband and his parents bought a falling-down Polish manor house. Though originally built in the early nineteenth century, Chobielin had been confiscated by the Communist regime in 1945, and abandoned and neglected afterward. The windows were broken, the floorboards were rotten, and the roof had caved in. As we started the reconstruction work, we discovered that the beams in the ground floor ceilings had to be replaced; later one of the cellar roof beams caved in, too.

Over the better part of a decade, we rebuilt, repainted, and restored. We also replanted the kitchen garden—or rather, my mother-in-law replanted the kitchen garden. She instinctively planted all of the vegetables that are always found in a Polish garden: beets, potatoes, carrots, parsnips, red cabbage, leeks, onions, yellow beans, squash, pumpkin, dill, radishes (both the small red ones and the long white ones), plus raspberries, strawberries, rhubarb, and currants (red currants and black ones). In the makeshift greenhouse—it's now been rebuilt, and is somewhat more professional—she planted tomatoes. In the small orchard—now not so small—she planted apple trees, pear trees, walnut trees, cherry trees, and plums. The latter, in particular, are now abundant producers of fruit.

Over the years, we sometimes added to this list. One summer, inspired by a visit to a seed market in Holland, I brought over a half dozen different kinds of lettuce. Not all of them took to the soil. But arugula, as it turned out, grew beautifully: Planted inside the greenhouse, it can be grown through October, and

one year we ate some at a late November Thanksgiving lunch I made for visiting American friends. It goes brilliantly with summer chicken salad, as well as with winter roasts. Some years we've had Swiss chard, some years spinach, and some years blueberries, too.

There is nothing revolutionary about throwing new ingredients into Polish cuisine. It's happened before: Poland is flat, and thus easy for invading armies to march across. Historically, Poles also had a fondness for foreign queens and imported monarchs. This means that foreign influences—Russian, German, Swedish, French, Italian, Hungarian, and even English—can all be found in Polish cooking, as in Polish culture. Bona Sforza, an Italian queen, is alleged to have brought the first soup vegetables to Poland. The influence of France—both the French aristocracy and, later, the French revolutionary circles frequented by Polish exiles in the nineteenth century—can be seen in the use of mustard sauces. And of course it is hard to say where Polish food ends and Ukrainian or Russian food begins, so similar are the tastes and ingredients.

In northwest Poland—our region is known as Kujawy, or western Pomerania—we also have our own local ingredients. Wild mushrooms grow in the woods around our house. In the past, we kept a few deer and had our own venison. Now we rely on friends for it—a neighbor has a deer farm—as well as wild boar and wild geese. Nearby fish farms breed trout, perch, and carp, and we can get salmon from the Baltic as well as smoked eel. Down the road, another neighbor keeps ducks and chickens in her barnyard which are, by definition, super-organic: They run free, eat insects, make a lot of noise, and taste delicious. So do their eggs, which we buy every week. Once, she apologized to me because they still had feathers sticking to them. I told her that in America, you pay extra for eggs with feathers, but I don't think she believed me.

Of course we cannot, in our Polish country house, reproduce the vast selection of exotic, out-of-season fruits and vegetables that one can find, nowadays, in a Western supermarket, or even a Warsaw supermarket, let alone the wide range of frozen meats and fish. Even though we now have Tesco (a British supermarket) and Carrefours (a French one) in the neighborhood, they don't have the same range of goods as their counterparts would in London or Paris.

The limited choices in the markets, especially when we first bought the manor house, in a way has been an advantage. Working with ingredients that were local, fresh, and available, I learned how to cook food that was, if not exactly traditional, then at least in the Polish spirit. The Polish combinations of meat and dried fruit, of wild mushrooms and kasha, of sour soups and spicy sausage, of homemade jams and pickles—all of those began to make sense. We didn't have fresh berries out of season, so I learned how to make sauces with red currant jam. We didn't have delicate summer vegetables all year-round, so I learned how to roast root vegetables in the winter. And thus, without really thinking about it, I learned how to cook.

❋ ❋ ❋

At the time, none of this seemed especially radical. But in 2009, a group of my American friends came to visit and discovered Polish cooking for the first time. They'd heard of kielbasa, but didn't know about *chłodnik*, cold beet soup. They'd run into cabbage rolls, but none of them knew about the game dishes or the wild mushrooms. And naturally, none had ever had the opportunity to taste the difference between a really fresh pickle and a pickle from a jar.

One of these friends was, of course, Danielle. As she notes in her preface to this book, she spent a few days in my house, carefully inspected my garden, went to a few restaurants, and made her declaration: The Polish culinary revolution had taken place. Now it was time to record the revolution for posterity. This cookbook was in fact Danielle's idea, and it reflects her aesthetic, literary, and culinary tastes as much as it does mine.

Neither of us would deny that the recipes that follow have a somewhat idiosyncratic character. We've changed some traditional Polish foods to suit our own tastes: The combination of beets with balsamic vinegar is sublime, and thus you will find a beet soup made with it here, even though that's not the way beets have been eaten in Poland for the past several centuries. Arugula appears here, too, as already noted, as does the odd foreign ingredient.

Danielle has also expanded on my own cooking experiences by using ingredients purchased at her local American grocery store, just to make sure they can be carried out even if you don't happen to live in a Polish country house. She has made several original contributions as well, not least by re-creating some of the recipes found in her husband David's Polish-Jewish family.

Both of us are intrigued by the overlap between Polish and Jewish food—as well as the overlap between Polish and Jewish culture—and have tried to explore it as much as possible. The first time I was ever invited to a Polish Easter breakfast, I was amazed by the many parallels with Passover. Both holidays celebrate eggs, both include symbols of rebirth and spring, and at both holiday tables you are likely to find beets, horseradish, and other spring vegetables. One of my Polish friends often serves *karp po żydowsku*—gefilte fish—for her Easter breakfast, which is about the most traditional Passover dish there is.

Finally, Danielle took it upon herself to tackle some of the most terrifying (to outsiders) Polish recipes, including pierogi, *barszcz* (beet soup), and cabbage rolls. She simplified, lightened, and reworked several of these Polish classics for the benefit of Anglo—or Polish—cooks. At one point during the course of this project, she unexpectedly found herself being filmed by a group of Polish television journalists while making duck and cabbage pierogi in her Washington kitchen. Not only did they love them, they asked her for the recipe. This was an early clue that we were on to a good thing.

Danielle and I both relied on other cookbooks, to compare and contrast the classic recipes and to see how things might be altered or fixed. The Polish books I used most often for reference were the basic but encyclopedic *Kuchnia Polska*, published by Swiat Ksiazki, and Hanna Szymanderska's wonderful and original *Polska Kuchnia Tradycjna*. In English, Danielle relied on Marja

Ochorowicz-Monatowa's *Polish Cookery*. I consulted Darra Goldstein's *A Taste of Russia* for a few recipes of Russian or Ukrainian origin. Astute cookbook readers will also detect the odd influence from Sheila Lukins's and Julee Rosso's classic *The New Basics Cookbook*, which was for a long time the only English-language cookbook I had in my Polish kitchen, as well as Nigella Lawson's first cookbook, *How to Eat*. Finally, for the flavored vodkas, I carefully perused the *Wielka Księga Nalewek* ("The Big Book of Flavored Vodkas") for relevant advice.

We've also relied on some friends. Three superb bakers—Meghan Gurdon in Washington, DC, Alison Kelso in London, and Beata Jerzy in Bydgoszcz—helped us test our cakes. One or two of our favorite Polish restaurants kicked in a recipe, and are acknowledged in the text. Both my mother-in-law, Teresa Sikorska, and a longtime family friend, Romka Kachelska, helped cook during the photo session and passed on tips. In fact, our photographers, Bogdan and Dorota Biały, are both wonderful cooks and very knowledgeable about Polish food as well. We consider ourselves lucky to have worked with them. Danielle's Washington butcher, Pam Ginsburg of Wagshal's, was an indefatigable and helpful source when it came to sourcing game, as well as figuring out cuts of meat that weren't specified in the original, often vague recipes.

We have, as our fiercer readers will note, left out some traditional stalwarts. *Flaki*, or tripe, a beloved national dish, is not in this book, as the thought of it didn't really appeal to our urban palates. Neither did *czernina*, duck blood soup. Other dishes fell by the wayside because they couldn't be reproduced in an American kitchen. *Kaszanka*—a kind of sausage made from meat and kasha, and one of my all-time favorite rural meals—is not here either for that reason, and we gave up on carp as well. The reader will not find baked ham here either. Neither one of us makes it, just because we don't.

But then, the point of this cookbook isn't to be authoritative. Our intention, rather, is to transmit some of the smells and tastes of the Polish countryside— a part of Europe that is still a little bit wilder, a little bit less well-groomed, and a little bit more primitive than the countryside in the lands to the West—and in doing so, to teach our readers to love it as much as we have come to do.

—Anne Applebaum

CHAPTER ONE

Appetizers
and
Starters

Caviar and Blini
BLINY Z KAWIOREM
page 42

Eggplant Caviar
KAWIOR Z BAKŁAŻANA
page 46

Herring, Two Ways
DWA SPOSOBY NA ŚLEDZIA
page 48

**Herring with Sour Cream
and Apples**
page 49

**Herring with Lime and
Raspberries**
page 50

Steak Tartare
BEFSZYK TATARSKI
page 53

Caviar and Blini

BLINY Z KAWIOREM

Makes 36 blinis

Once upon a time, sturgeon swam in the Vistula River and Poles ate caviar in abundance, just as the English working classes once ate oysters. Nowadays most caviar eaten in Poland comes from Russia, and more specifically from the Volga River. The Volga is—or used to be—one of the world's greatest breeding grounds for sturgeon, the ugly, prehistoric, bottom-dwelling fish whose black eggs have been strained, salted, and eaten since ancient times. Aristotle mentions caviar, the Persians believed it had medicinal properties, and many have considered it an aphrodisiac. But of course caviar is associated above all with the Russian czars, who personally controlled the rights to gather sturgeon caviar in Russia, and who insouciantly served vast platters of it at their banquets. In the nineteenth century, what is now eastern Poland—including the cities of Warsaw, Lublin, and Białystok—was a part of the Russian Empire, so the cachet of caviar was preserved.

Not that serving caviar at banquets died out in the Soviet era. On the contrary, caviar remained a symbol of privilege and wealth in Soviet Russia—and in the Soviet Empire's satellite states, of which Poland was one—all the more so because one could no longer buy it without connections. To serve it, in fact, was a kind of statement: The hostess who could produce caviar was a hostess who had friends in high places. Thus it became a staple at higher Communist Party functions.

The Soviet Union party bosses controlled sturgeon fishing as tightly as their czarist predecessors. But this was not entirely out of selfishness. By definition, the harvesting of caviar—which involves catching and killing pregnant fish in order to remove their egg sacs—can destroy a sturgeon population very quickly if it is not strictly limited and controlled. And destruction was indeed the result when the Soviet Union collapsed, and caviar control collapsed along with it. Sturgeon was overfished, caviar was overharvested, and production dwindled.

But for one brief and extraordinary historical moment, caviar—even the very best beluga caviar—was amazingly cheap and easily available across Eastern Europe, especially in Poland. In fact, in the early 1990s, Warsaw was probably the world's best place to buy it: Russian traders were then visiting the city in droves, looking to sell things for hard currency. The city already had open farmers' markets, and one of them, on Polna Street, became the place to buy caviar. On a good day, a small tin of beluga could be purchased for five or

continued

ten dollars, at a time when the cost in London or Paris was ten or twenty times that much. At that price, it made sense for Viennese restaurateurs to fly in for the day just to buy caviar, and some of them did.

Anne started eating and serving caviar back then, when it was so plentiful you could throw it in your breakfast scrambled eggs without feeling much guilt. Now it is once again as expensive in Poland as anywhere else, and when she gets some—usually as a present from a Russian friend—it's a great occasion. There is a chance that will change; sturgeon farming is becoming more common, not only in Central Europe but also in the United States. Reportedly, it is now possible to find caviar from the West Coast that is just as good as the "real thing."

Caviar can be served without any ornament or additions whatsoever, in a silver dish, with nothing but slices of white toast. It can also be dressed up and made elaborate. Anne's mother used to make a caviar "pie" with sour cream and chopped egg. Caviar is also sometimes served with lemon, red onion, and capers, just like smoked salmon is often served in New York, though we both find caviar too delicate for these strong tastes. Danielle has been known to serve caviar with her latkes at Chanukah. But our favorite way to serve caviar happens to be the most traditional: with blinis and sour cream.

There are many blini recipes, some very rich, involving sour cream and sugar, and some not much different from ordinary pancakes. This recipe falls some-where in the middle. It does use yeast—true blinis are always made with yeast—but this needn't intimidate the first-time blini maker; there's not much yeast and it does make the dough extraordinarily fluffy. This recipe also calls for a mix of buckwheat and plain white wheat flour, which gives the blinis some heft without making them heavy. We also use milk and not sour cream as specified in some batters, because the sour cream is meant to go on top, after all, underneath the caviar.

As for the caviar, buy as much as you can afford, or as much as you can find. Black caviar is far more expensive, and beluga—which has much larger eggs and a jellylike texture—is the most expensive black caviar. But the three other traditional types—sevruga, sterlet, and ossetra, each laid by a different type of sturgeon—also have their proponents. For the record, the eggs of sterlet caviar are smaller and almost golden; ossetra is brownish, and almost as highly valued as beluga; gray sevruga is the cheapest. But the distinctions among them are minor, quite frankly, unless you are a true connoisseur. As noted, there are many non-Russian caviars now worth trying—especially American—but be careful always to buy sturgeon eggs and not lumpfish. Don't forget red salmon caviar, which is much cheaper, and which Russians and Poles rate just as highly. Anne served blinis with red caviar at a recent New Year's Eve party, and it was the highlight of the evening.

¼ cup/60 ml warm water (105 to 115°F/40 to 45°C)

One ¼-oz/7-g package active dry yeast (2¼ tsp)

1½ tsp sugar

½ cup/65 g sifted all-purpose flour

½ cup/60 g sifted buckwheat flour

¼ tsp salt

1 cup/240 ml warm whole milk (105 to 115°F/40 to 45°C)

4 tbsp/55 g unsalted butter, melted and cooled

2 large eggs, lightly beaten

Sour cream for serving

Caviar, red or black, as much as you feel up to serving

Preheat the oven to 250°F/120°C/gas ½.

Combine the warm water, yeast, and sugar in a medium mixing bowl and let stand until the yeast gets foamy, about 5 minutes. (If it doesn't foam, start over with fresh yeast.)

Stir in the two flours and salt, and then the milk, 3 tbsp of the butter, and the eggs. Cover the bowl with plastic wrap and set in a roasting pan filled with 1 in/2.5 cm of warm water. Let rise in a warm place until the dough has increased in volume, has a bubbly surface, and is stringy when scooped up (about 1½ to 2 hours).

When the batter is ready, brush some of the remaining 1 tbsp butter in a large frying pan over medium-high heat. If the butter browns, lower the heat immediately. Working in batches of four blinis, spoon 1 tbsp of batter into the pan for each one. Cook until golden brown on each side, about 2 minutes per side. Transfer cooked blinis to an ovenproof platter and keep warm in the oven while you make the remaining blinis.

These can be plated—three or four blinis with a dollop of sour cream and a few heaping spoonfuls of caviar on each plate—or served in a happy pile beside a large mound of caviar set on ice with a side dish of sour cream. Take your pick.

Eggplant Caviar

KAWIOR Z BAKŁAŻANA

Serves 10 to 12

In the Communist era, eggplant was not readily available in Poland, but it seems to have made its way back with a vengeance. Piles of purple eggplants appear in street markets in the late summer, and Anne has eaten them grilled at a Polish campfire. This is a more sophisticated suggestion: A recipe for eggplant "caviar" that is served in both Russia and Poland as an hors d'oeuvre or as a *zakuski*, a kind of snack eaten with vodka. Eggplant caviar is found in French and Mediterranean cooking, but we suspect that the true ethnic origins of this particular recipe are Georgian. It certainly has the sharpness and flavor that everyone in the region associates with Georgian food (and with Georgian politics), both of which appeal to Poland's romantic sensibility. During the short Russian-Georgian war in 2008, Georgian wines and Georgian food suddenly appeared on Polish restaurant menus. The corner store where Anne sometimes picked up groceries in Warsaw suddenly began selling Borjomi, a famous brand of Georgian mineral water, which tastes somewhat metallic but is supposed to be extremely healthful. They displayed bottles of it prominently on the counter. We include this recipe in memory of that moment of solidarity.

For an hors d'oeuvre, pass the caviar spread on crackers. It can also be served as a first course, in small dollops on toast points. If you've made too much to consume before a meal, then serve it as a side dish (at room temperature), alongside meat or fish.

> 3 small eggplants (about 2¼ lb/1 kg)
> ½ cup/120 ml olive oil
> 2 medium onions, finely chopped
> 1 green bell pepper, finely chopped
> 4 garlic cloves, crushed and minced
> 3 large and juicy tomatoes, peeled and finely chopped,
> or 3 cups/795 g canned peeled tomatoes, drained and chopped
> Generous 1 tsp honey
> Salt and freshly ground pepper
> Juice of 1 lemon

Preheat the oven to 375°F/190°C/gas 5. Place the whole eggplants in a shallow roasting pan and bake until tender, about 45 minutes. Let cool.

Meanwhile, in a large frying pan, warm the olive oil over medium heat and cook the onions until soft but not brown. Add the bell pepper and garlic. Keep cooking until the bell pepper is soft.

After the eggplants have cooled, cut them in half and scoop out the pulp. Discard the skins. Chop up the pulp and add to the frying pan along with the tomatoes and honey. Season with 1 tbsp salt and pepper. Cover, lower the heat, and simmer for about 1 hour, until the ingredients are thoroughly soft and melded. Uncover the pan to let the excess liquid evaporate, and cook, stirring occasionally, for about 20 minutes, depending on the liquidity of the vegetables. Squeeze in as much of the lemon juice as you'd like, and check the seasoning. Add more salt and pepper if necessary.

Transfer the "caviar" to a bowl and refrigerate overnight.

Herring, Two Ways

DWA SPOSOBY NA ŚLEDZIA

Pickled herring is most definitely an acquired taste. Anne's husband, Radek, who was made to eat all kinds of canned and pickled fish as a child (this was the late Communist period, his father was a fanatical fisherman, and there wasn't much choice) will not touch it. But those who love it truly love it. It is the combination of sweet and salty, more than anything else, that makes herring unique, as well as the fact that it can be served in so many ways.

Herring can be served cold, with onions, peppers, and tomato sauce, as a kind of antipasto. It can also be eaten simply, on toast, for breakfast. In Sweden—just across the Baltic from Poland, and a major culinary and cultural influence, especially in the port city of Gdansk—several kinds of herring are often served at once, alongside many other dishes, at Christmas smorgasbords. Herring can also be served with chopped raw onions and olive oil alongside warm potatoes for lunch, which is how it is eaten at our favorite seaside restaurants in Jastarnia and Jurata, on the Polish Baltic coast. Perhaps for that reason, the very taste of it brings to mind the white sand, fresh wind, and pine trees of the Hel Peninsula, a spit of land that juts into the Baltic, east of Gdansk, and has some of the most beautiful beaches we've ever seen.

When shopping for herring, it's best to look for matyas (or matjes) herring, which has been soaked or "soused" in a low-salt brine and is very soft and mild. Herring preserved this way is usually marked as such and if you ask for it, a good delicatessen will know what you mean. Herring pickled in vinegar is much sharper in taste, and doesn't combine so easily with other ingredients. The usual way to eat vinegar-pickled herring is in the form of a rollmop: a small piece of fish wrapped around an olive or some capers, and eaten with a toothpick as an hors d'oeuvre or a snack to go with beer or vodka. Raw herrings can also be poached, fried, or grilled. But the soused version is what one wants for these salads.

The first recipe is a modern version of a classic herring "salad," which Anne was served as a first course at a dinner party organized by her friend Agata Bielik-Robson, a professor of philosophy in Warsaw. When Anne asked for the recipe, Agata told Anne that she didn't think there was such a thing as a recipe; all she could offer was "the ingredients in an approximate proportions." Following is our interpretation of her description of them. The dish would also work well as part of a lunch or brunch buffet. And we note, for the record, that the inclusion of garlic inspires a certain amount of controversy in Poland, where some people would never use it, while others can't imagine this dish without it. We've left it in, but it's your choice.

Herring with Sour Cream and Apples

Serves 4

14 oz/400 g matyas (matjes) fillets of herring

1 large apple ("of a rather sweet sort," says Agata, perhaps Fuji
or Gala), peeled and diced

3 large eggs, hard-boiled and sliced into thin rounds

1 medium seedless cucumber, peeled and diced

3 to 4 medium sour dill pickles, sliced thin

1 tbsp light mayonnaise

1 cup/240 ml sour cream (nonfat is fine if you prefer it)

2 tbsp chopped fresh basil

2 garlic cloves, crushed and minced

Freshly ground pepper

Fresh black bread or crisp white toast for serving

Cut the herring into bite-size chunks and put in a large bowl. Add the apple, eggs, cucumber, pickles, mayonnaise, sour cream, basil, and garlic. Season with pepper and mix. You won't need salt; the herring is already salty enough. Agata writes that you then let the salad acquire "bite" in the refrigerator for about 1 hour. "And that's all."

Serve with the bread of your choice.

Herring with Lime and Raspberries

Serves 4

This is a more elegant, less traditional way to eat herring. Somehow it preserves the sweet-and-sour, fruity-fishy spirit of the classic version, and yet has a fresher taste, reminiscent of ceviche. There is no cream in this recipe, which makes it an even lighter and more elegant first course.

> 2 sweet apples, peeled and coarsely grated
> Juice of 1 lime, plus 1½ tsp grated lime zest
> 1 tsp white wine vinegar
> 4 matyas (matjes) fillets of herring
> 1 cup/140 g fresh raspberries, plus more for garnish

Mix the grated apple with the lime juice and vinegar in a small bowl. Place the herring fillets in a small dish, spread the mixture on top, and marinate for 4 hours. (If not consuming within 4 hours, refrigerate for up to 12 hours. Bring to room temperature before continuing.) Remove the fillets and wipe off the marinade, reserving the marinade. Place the fillets on a serving dish.

Pour the apple marinade into a blender, add the 1 cup/140 g raspberries and the lime zest and blend until smooth. Drizzle the mixture over the herring, garnish with the remaining raspberries, and serve.

Steak Tartare

BEFSZYK TATARSKI

Serves 4

According to legend, steak tartare is named after the Tatars, nomadic horsemen who, at the battle of Grunwald in 1410, famously sided with the Polish king against the Germanic Teutonic Knights. The Poles won that battle, which marked the beginning of the rise of the Polish-Lithuanian Commonwealth, a loose empire that ruled eastern Central Europe until the end of the eighteenth century. The Tatars, though Muslim, had special status in the empire, and a few Tatar villages still survive in eastern Poland. Allegedly, the Tatar warriors ate raw meat because they had no time to stop and cook; they are said to have tenderized the meat by carrying it all day under their saddles.

You don't have to be a nomadic horseman to eat delicate bits of fresh uncooked prime beef, carefully prepared. Steak tartare is served in all the capitals of Central Europe; the Italians eat uncooked beef in the form of carpaccio. This recipe for steak tartare was generously given to us by one of our favorite Warsaw restaurants, U Kucharze—a part of the Gessler family empire. Built in the former basement kitchen of the old Hotel Europejski, U Kucharze retains a 1930s semi-industrial kitchen aesthetic. There are white tiles on the floor, sinks on the walls; the cooks stand in the middle of the restaurant and shout at one another while elegant Warsovians dine around them. The "napkins" are linen dish towels—and the food is superb. We almost always order the steak tartare, not least because the cooks prepare it at the table, and watching them chop all the ingredients together is half the fun.

The recipe is easily doubled or halved.

> 1 lb/455 g filet mignon trimmed of any visible fat
> (The meat should be very fresh and of good quality.)
> 2 large eggs (ideally farm-fresh, if you can get them)
> 2 medium sour dill pickles, diced
> 1 medium onion, diced
> 1 tsp capers, finely chopped if large
> 2 garlic cloves, diced
> Salt and freshly ground pepper

continued

Rinse the meat, pat dry, and then mince. This is traditionally done with two sharp knives, but it can also be done with a food processor. Just don't overprocess. You can ask a butcher to do this as well.

Flatten the pile of beef gently on a cutting board. Crack the eggs on top and work them in as evenly and thoroughly as possible. At U Kucharze they do this with two knives. I've found it's easier with two forks: turn the meat over again and again until the eggs are absorbed. Continue to add each ingredient in the same manner, one by one, thoroughly incorporating the first before adding the next. Season with salt and pepper.

Divide the meat evenly into four portions. At U Kucharze, each serving is shaped into three elegant ovals per plate, which you can do by pressing the meat into a soup spoon and overturning it.

Eat immediately—the steak needs no other accompaniment.

CHAPTER TWO

Soups

Sour Cucumber Soup
OGÓRKOWA
page 60

Beet Soup, Three Ways
BARSZCZ
page 63

Traditional Barszcz
page 64

A Jazzier Barszcz
page 65

Summer Beet Soup
CHŁODNIK
page 67

Two Wild Mushroom Soups
ZUPA GRZYBOWA
page 69

Traditional Zupa Grzybowa
page 71

A Boozier Zupa Grzybowa
page 72

Sorrel Soup
ZUPA SZCZAWIOWA
page 75

Sour Bread Soup, or White Barszcz
ŻUREK, ALBO "BARSZCZ BIAŁY"
page 78

Chicken Soup
ROSÓŁ
page 80

Foolproof Matzoh Balls
KNEJDLACH
page 84

Dripped Noodles
LANE KLUSKI
page 86

Next-Day Tomato Soup
ZUPA POMIDOROWA
page 87

Mustard Soup
ZUPA MUSZTARDOWA
page 88

Split Pea Soup
GROCHÓWKA
page 90

Sour Cucumber Soup

OGÓRKOWA

Serves 6

In Poland, when they talk about cucumber soup, they don't mean the pallid white stuff. *Ogórkowa* is made with sour cucumbers—otherwise known as dill pickles. The idea of pickle soup may seem counterintuitive. What on earth is it supposed to taste like, you might wonder. A condiment? But in fact it is nothing more than a tastier, earthier, "dillier" version of its effete fresh cucumber cousin. Obviously this works better if you have your own homemade sour pickles, but good sour dill pickles—not the sweet kind—from a jar are fine, too. They don't have to be kosher dills, but those are often high quality.

Our recipe comes from a Polish friend of Danielle's, Włodek Szemberg, who first introduced her to the exotic possibilities of Polish cuisine by serving her this soup at a dinner party more than two decades ago; the memory of its surprise and deliciousness remained strong. The result is hearty and deeply fragrant of dill. Served with dark bread and butter, it makes a complete meal.

> 1 tbsp unsalted butter
>
> 1 medium leek (white and green parts),
> trimmed, rinsed, and chopped into ½-in/12-mm pieces
>
> 1 medium carrot, trimmed, peeled, and chopped into ½-in/
> 12-mm pieces
>
> 1 medium parsnip, peeled and chopped into ½-in/12-mm pieces
>
> ½ medium celery root, peeled, or 2 celery stalks, trimmed;
> chopped into ½-in/12-mm pieces
>
> 5 cups/1.2 L chicken stock
>
> 3 large baking potatoes, peeled and chopped into ½-in/12-mm
> pieces
>
> One 32-oz/910-g jar sour dill pickles and their brine
>
> Salt and freshly ground pepper
>
> ¼ cup/60 ml heavy cream
>
> Generous 2 tbsp chopped fresh dill

In a medium soup pot, melt the butter over medium heat. Add the leek and cook until softened. Add the carrot, parsnip, and celery root to the soup pot; pour in the chicken stock; and bring to a boil. Cover, lower the heat, and simmer for 30 minutes or until the vegetables are tender.

Place the potatoes in a separate pot, cover with water, and boil until they are cooked but still slightly firm, approximately 7 or 8 minutes. Drain and set aside.

In the meantime, strain the pickle brine and reserve it. Coarsely grate the pickles using a cheese grater or the grater attachment on a food processor. After the vegetables have simmered, add the pickles to the soup pot, as well as all their brine, and the cooked potatoes. Season with salt and pepper, and simmer for an additional 5 minutes. Use an immersion blender to purée the soup in the pot, or whizz it lightly in a blender or food processor (you want the end result to still be a little chunky, not whipped smooth). Mix in the heavy cream. Add the chopped dill just before serving.

Beet Soup, Three Ways

BARSZCZ

Barszcz, or beet soup, is perhaps best known around the world by its Russian name, *borscht*, but versions of both the soup and the word are part of every Slavic culture. Either dark purple or bright pink—if you add sour cream—*barszcz* is a winter staple across Central and Eastern Europe. (The summer version, cold beet soup, is known in Polish as *chłodnik*; see page 67).

At its best, *barszcz* is a classic sweet-and-sour dish, with the beet providing the sweetness and lemon juice or vinegar providing an acidic note. Like chicken soup, *barszcz* is alleged to have healing powers. When a friend of ours first had chemotherapy, we brought him a thermos of *barszcz*, which he claimed made him feel better, so perhaps it is true.

Traditional country-house *barszcz* is really a stock made with beef or veal bones and beets, carefully strained and served crystal clear, sometimes with a *pasteczik*, a small savory pastry filled with meat or cabbage, on the side. Other versions call for the beets to be grated and served with the soup. Still others insist on the addition of small dumplings (*uszki*, which means "little ears"). It is not unusual in Polish restaurants to be given the choice of several versions of *barszcz*.

We are including two versions of *barszcz* here: one more traditional and one jazzed up by, among other things, the addition of balsamic vinegar. Both versions are extremely low in fat (unless you like lots of sour cream), very cheap, and ridiculously easy.

When peeling beets (raw or cooked), it's best to wear rubber or disposable surgical gloves, unless you like having the tips of your fingers dyed bright pink.

continued

Traditional Barszcz

Serves 6 to 8 as an appetizer, or 4 to 6 as a main course

4 large or 6 small beets, peeled and halved
1 lb/455 g meaty veal or beef bones
1 medium carrot, trimmed and peeled
1 medium parsnip, trimmed and peeled
1 large onion, peeled and halved
1 leek (white and green parts), trimmed, halved lengthwise, and rinsed
¼ celery root, peeled, or 1 long celery stalk
3 to 4 dried mushrooms or porcini, if you've got them
8 garlic cloves, peeled but left whole, plus 2 extra just in case
1 bay leaf
1 large pinch of dried marjoram, plus more for seasoning
6 peppercorns (optional; throw them in if you like a spicier soup)
About 12 cups/2.8 L water (depending on the size of the pot)
Juice of 1 lemon
Salt and freshly ground pepper
½ cup/120 ml sour cream or plain Greek-style yogurt (optional)

Combine the beets, bones, carrot, parsnip, onion, leek, celery root, mushrooms, 8 garlic cloves, the bay leaf, marjoram, peppercorns (if using), and water in a large stockpot and bring to a boil. (There should be enough water to cover the other ingredients.) Remove any foam that has risen to the top, cover, and turn down the heat. Simmer gently until the meat falls off the bones and the vegetables are very soft, about 2 hours.

Strain the soup through a colander, pressing the solids to extract all the liquids. Taste: If it is too watery, then boil down, uncovered, for an additional 30 minutes or so. If it seems too dense, add water. When the soup is ready, stir in the lemon juice. Season with salt and pepper and, if you like, some more dried marjoram.

You might also ask yourself at this point whether the soup needs even more garlic, in which case peel a couple more cloves, crush them with a garlic press or the flat side of a knife, toss them in, and simmer for a minute or two. Make sure they don't fall into anyone's bowl when you serve (unless, like Anne, the person happens to like boiled garlic cloves). The flavor should be slightly sour and garlicky, yet with that beety hint of sweetness.

Serve clear, very hot, in small bowls or even large teacups, which you can pick up and drink. If you prefer yours bright pink, then serve in large soup plates with a spoonful of the sour cream or plain yogurt dropped into each one. This keeps in the refrigerator (covered) for days, and indeed grows slightly tangier with time, which is how it is supposed to be.

A Jazzier Barszcz
Serves 6

As noted, *barszcz* is usually made with either vinegar or lemon juice, which adds an acidic dash to the sweetness of the beets. This soup, partly inspired by a recipe of Nigella Lawson's, takes that basic notion one step further and uses balsamic vinegar instead of the more traditional red wine vinegar. It is in fact more like a very thin, drinkable beet purée than an actual soup; it doesn't have a stock base, like traditional *barszcz*. But we can't see that it matters, since this recipe veers radically away from tradition anyway (balsamic vinegar has, after all, only been available in Poland in the past couple of decades). This soup is incredibly light and invigorating—perfect served cold on a very hot summer day, with a garlicky green salad, or boiling hot in the winter as a light first course.

> **About 4 qt/3.8 L water**
> **4 large or 6 small beets, peel left on, halved**
> **1 onion, peeled and halved**
> **3 garlic cloves, peeled**
> **1 tbsp balsamic vinegar**
> **Salt and freshly ground pepper**
> **½ cup/120 ml plain kefir if eating cold; ½ cup/120 ml sour cream if eating hot**

Fill a large stockpot with the water, and add the beets, onion, and garlic. Bring to a gentle boil and cook, uncovered, on low heat for a good hour, or longer if necessary, until the beets are soft. Remove the vegetables with a slotted spoon, and set the beet stock aside. Throw out the onion. Remove the skins from the beets by hand—they will now slip off easily—and place the beets in a blender with the garlic. Pulse until smooth. Return the puréed beets and garlic to the pot with their stock, and add the balsamic vinegar. Season with salt and pepper and stir. Add water if too thick, or boil down some more if too runny.

If eating cold, stir in the kefir just before serving, adding a spoonful to each bowl so that people can swish it around with their spoons. If eating hot, consider stirring in spoonfuls of sour cream instead.

This, like other *barszcz* recipes, will also keep for several days in the refrigerator and generally improve. Drink a glass of it, cold, for an abstemious lunch.

Summary Beet Soup
CHŁODNIK

Serves 6

It's hard to imagine a summer in the country without *chłodnik*: Icy cold, tasting of fresh dill and kefir (or light yogurt), with a glimmer of sweet beets and crunchy cucumbers. It is the most refreshing food you can possibly eat on a hot afternoon. The color—light pink, with flecks of green—is elegant enough to serve as the first course of a formal lunch, though *chłodnik* can also be eaten on its own as a light supper. The taste and texture contain echoes of Greek tzatziki and Spanish gazpacho, but the combination is thoroughly Polish. Although, just to confuse you, we will note that Poles often call this soup *chłodnik Litewski*, which means "Lithuanian *chłodnik*." That is one more testimony to the close relationship of Poland and Lithuania, which were bound together in a single state for many centuries.

As with many traditional dishes, there are many versions of *chłodnik*. We prefer a lighter version, made with kefir, if you can get it, or nonfat yogurt. We also like to use hard-boiled eggs, which give the soup some heft (for a more exotic touch, you may substitute hard-boiled quail's eggs). To be more specific, Anne prefers her mother-in-law's version, which has both kefir and eggs. But when Anne asked her for a recipe, she said she never measures anything and does it all "by eye." Danielle experimented with her approximations, and this is Danielle's attempt to quantify the perfect *chłodnik* for those of us not doing it "by eye."

2 to 3 medium beets, or 5 to 6 small beets
(Try to use very fresh beets, as these will produce the best color.)

2 medium cucumbers, peeled and cut into ¼-in/6-mm dice

1 small celery stalk, with leaves; stalks cut into ¼-in/6-mm dice, and leaves finely chopped

¼ cup plus 1 tbsp/10 g finely chopped fresh dill

¼ cup plus 1 tbsp/10 g finely chopped flat-leaf parsley

1 large bunch of fresh chives, finely chopped

1 tsp salt

1 tsp freshly ground pepper

Pinch of sugar

8 cups/2 L kefir or, if unavailable, plain nonfat yogurt

3 large eggs or 12 quail's eggs, hard-boiled
(Keep refrigerated until ready to serve.)

continued

In a large saucepan, cover the beets with water and boil until soft. Drain and let cool, and then remove the skins (they should slip off easily).

Cut the beets into relatively small, even dice, about ¼ in/6 mm. Toss the vegetables and herbs in a large bowl, together with the salt, pepper, and sugar.

Pour in the kefir (or yogurt), and mix all the ingredients in the bowl together well. Refrigerate for a few hours, preferably overnight. You will notice that the beets will have "bled"—creating bright pink streaks. Stir to even out the color, bearing in mind the summery blush is part of the soup's traditional charm. When ready to serve, peel and thinly slice the hard-boiled eggs (or halve the quail eggs, and use two eggs per serving). Mix the soup again just before serving, and ladle into individual bowls, placing the egg slices on top.

Two Wild Mushroom Soups

ZUPA GRZYBOWA

Most soups are successful because they blend the flavors of different vegetables with meat and spices. Wild mushroom soup is quite different: When it works, it works because it transmits the essence of wild mushrooms. In theory, nothing in a good wild mushroom soup should compete with their woodsy flavor. In Poland, wild mushroom soup sometimes goes under different names, depending upon which kind of mushroom is used: *borowikowa* (from *borowiki*, or boletes), for example, or *kurkowa* (from *kurki*, or chanterelles).

Unlike most Western versions of mushroom soup, *zupa grzybowa* is traditionally made without cream or meat. It is therefore eaten at Lent and very often on Christmas Eve, when Polish Catholics avoid meat. Because it is made with dried mushrooms, the soup can also be eaten all year-round, though it tends to be served in the winter or early spring, when fresh vegetables are scarce.

continued

Traditional Zupa Grzybowa

Serves 6 as an appetizer, or 4 as a main course

This is the traditional soup. Like *barszcz* (beet soup), it is in fact a stock, with the mushrooms taking the place of the chicken or beef. Soup vegetables provide a delicate background for the broth, but there is no seasoning except salt, pepper, and a bit of fresh dill. This version is inspired by a country neighbor of Anne's, Pani Pacholska—the wife of her brilliant carpenter—who would use even fewer vegetables than we do; however her ability to make perfect soup out of almost nothing except a handful of dried mushrooms requires thirty years of practice.

8 cups/2 L water

1 to 2 oz/30 to 55 g mixed dried wild mushrooms (porcini, morels, cèpes, and, if you can get them, *borowiki* or boletes)

1 medium onion, peeled and halved

1 medium carrot, trimmed and peeled

1 medium parsnip, trimmed and peeled

½ celery root, peeled and halved, or 2 celery stalks, trimmed

2 leeks (white part only), trimmed, halved lengthwise, rinsed, and cut into chunks (you will be removing them from the soup)

1 tbsp all-purpose flour

2 tbsp unsalted butter, melted

Handful of chopped fresh dill

Salt and freshly ground pepper

1 lb/455 g pearl barley, cooked according to the package directions (optional)

Pour the water into a soup pot. Rinse the dried mushrooms and leave them in the pot for several hours—overnight is best. When ready to cook, strain the water through a fine-mesh strainer lined with a paper towel or cheesecloth into a large bowl—this will remove any grit from the mushrooms. Press or squeeze out as much water as you can. Then rinse the mushrooms again and return the soaking water and mushrooms to the soup pot. Add the onion halves and bring to a boil. Add all the other vegetables. Bring to a boil again, cover, and simmer for 1 hour. Remove the carrot, parsnip, celery root, onion, and leeks. Leave in the mushrooms.

In a small bowl, stir the flour together with the melted butter to make a paste. Ladle 1 to 2 tbsp of the hot soup into the bowl, stirring until incorporated. Pour this mixture into the still simmering soup, whisking until dissolved and the soup has thickened.

Add the chopped dill, and season with salt and pepper. If you want to add some heft to the soup, place a portion of the cooked barley in each bowl before pouring the soup on top to serve. This gives the soup a little bit of crunch and adds a note of contrast.

A Boozier Zupa Grzybowa

Serves 6 as an appetizer, or 4 as a main course

As is so often the case with traditional Polish soups, there is another, more radical school of thought: Some believe that the indescribably perfect flavor of wild mushrooms can actually be enhanced with one or two other tastes. Even more radically, some believe mushroom soup needn't be thin and ethereal, but might also be chunky and rich. Our second soup recipe thus adds Madeira (or port) as well as ordinary cultivated mushrooms to the mix. The former gives it a more sophisticated taste, the latter some extra bulk. Anne always uses wild mushroom stock here as well; it can be purchased either fresh or as bouillon cubes. Or you can make it yourself by simmering the "traditional" recipe on page 71 for a total of 3 hours, uncovered. If you can't get or make mushroom stock, then substitute beef stock, which works almost as well.

½ cup/120 ml Madeira (we have also used port successfully)

3 cups/720 ml chicken stock

1 oz/30 g mixed dried wild mushrooms (porcini, morels, cèpes, and boletes)

4 tbsp/55 g unsalted butter

3 leeks (white and light green parts), trimmed, rinsed, and diced

1 medium onion, peeled and diced

1 cup/225 g fresh cultivated mushrooms, cleaned, halved lengthwise, and tough parts of stems removed

3 tbsp all-purpose flour

2 cups/480 ml mushroom stock, or if unavailable, beef stock

Salt and freshly ground pepper

1 cup/240 ml crème fraîche

Handful of chopped fresh dill

In a small saucepan, combine the Madeira, ½ cup/120 ml of the chicken stock, and the dried mushrooms. Bring to a boil and then immediately remove from the heat. Let sit for at least 30 minutes. Strain the mixture through a fine-mesh strainer lined with a paper towel or cheesecloth set over a bowl to remove any grit from the stock. Press any extra water from the mushrooms, then rinse the mushrooms well. Return to the bowl with the strained stock, and set aside.

In the meantime, melt the butter in a soup pot and cook the leeks and onion over medium heat until soft, about 10 minutes. Add the fresh mushrooms and continue to cook until the mushrooms glisten and sweat a little, another few minutes or so. Sprinkle with the flour and stir until mixed well. Pour in the Madeira and dried mushroom mixture, stirring constantly so the broth thickens without curdling. Gradually pour in the remaining 2½ cups/600 ml of chicken stock and the mushroom stock, continuing to stir. Season with salt and pepper. Raise the heat, bring to a boil, and then immediately lower the heat to a simmer. Simmer, uncovered, until all mushrooms are cooked, about 30 minutes.

Use an immersion blender to purée the soup in the pot, but only partially; leave some of the mushroom chunks intact. This should not be a perfect purée. Serve, adding a dollop of crème fraîche and a sprinkle of fresh dill to each bowl.

Sorrel Soup

ZUPA SZCZAWIOWA

Serves 4 to 6

Anne discovered the glories of sorrel one summer when she accidentally planted too much of it. If this fortunate misfortune has not befallen you yet, then it's time for you to discover sorrel, too. It looks like a simple green lettuce leaf, but when cooked, it reduces quickly to almost a lemony puddle—perfect for buttery, citrusy sauces and soups.

With what seemed like a forest of sorrel to dispense of—and quickly —Anne made pot after pot of sorrel soup, each one a bit different. This version was the one she finally settled upon. The lemon preserves the color and the citrus flavor; the arugula tones it down and makes the final result less acidic. Anne has encountered a version of sorrel soup in Hungary that is sweet, which she did not like at all: Sugar gave it a sickly, syrupy flavor, which was unpleasant. The Polish version hints at lemons and citrus fruit, and isn't sweet.

We often put a halved hard-boiled egg or one or two halved hard-boiled quail's eggs into each bowl of sorrel soup, which gives it a protein boost. And for the chilled version, an elegant way to serve it is with parsley ice cubes: To make the ice cubes, fill an ice tray with water. To each "cube" add the top of a fresh parsley sprig, to give the appearance of a sprig floating in ice. You can also finely chop a handful of fresh parsley and sprinkle it among the cubes. Freeze and when ready to serve, float an ice cube in the center of each bowl, alongside the egg if using.

continued

4 tbsp/55 g unsalted butter

1 onion, peeled and coarsely chopped

1 carrot, trimmed, peeled, and coarsely chopped

½ celery root, peeled, and chopped, or 2 celery stalks, trimmed and chopped

1 leek (white part only), trimmed, rinsed, and thickly sliced

4 garlic cloves, peeled

½ lb/225 g sorrel leaves

½ lb/225 g arugula

4 cups/960 ml chicken stock

½ cup/20 g chopped fresh flat-leaf parsley

2 tsp nutmeg, freshly grated if possible

Salt and freshly ground pepper

Juice of ½ lemon

About ⅜ cup/90 ml plain yogurt (low-fat is fine) for cold soup, or heavy cream for hot

6 eggs—or 6 to 12 quail's eggs, if you can get them—hard-boiled, peeled and halved, for garnish (optional)

In a large soup pot, melt the butter over medium heat and cook the onion, carrot, celery root, leek, and garlic together until the onion is soft. Add the sorrel and arugula, and let simmer for 5 minutes. Add the chicken stock, parsley, and nutmeg; season with salt and pepper; and bring to a boil. Then lower the heat and let simmer on very low heat for 1 hour, uncovered. Stir occasionally and add a little extra broth if the soup reduces too much.

When done, let the soup cool. Stir in the lemon juice. Blend the ingredients with an immersion blender—or for a creamier texture, a food processor—until the soup is completely smooth.

If you're planning on serving the soup cold, refrigerate. When ready to serve, season with salt and pepper, and add a dollop of yogurt to each bowl. Pour the soup over the yogurt and garnish with the eggs, yolk-side up (if using). For hot soup, season a little more heavily with the salt and pepper, omit the yogurt, and add a splash of heavy cream to each serving. Garnish with eggs, if desired.

Sour Bread Soup, or White Barszcz

ŻUREK, ALBO "BARSZCZ BIAŁY"

Serves 4 to 6

In its way, *żurek*—pronounced "zhurek"—is the most humble of all Polish soups, and at the same time the most exotic, at least to the foreign palate. It has traditionally been eaten at Easter, but now is found on menus all year-round. Though distantly related to the bread and garlic soups of Spain and Italy, its base is not meat or vegetable broth, but *zakwas*. *Zakwas* is made from rye bread and water and is, in turn, distantly related both to sourdough and to Russian *kvass* (a fermented drink). In Poland, *zakwas* is available in bottles at ordinary supermarkets. Outside of Poland, you can find it in specialty ethnic markets, and even online. If you do have to make it yourself, although it sounds odd and intimidating, it is in fact extremely easy. But it does require planning a few days in advance.

Żurek can be thin and delicate or hearty, stuffed with chunks of ham, sausage, and potatoes—in which case it is really an entire meal. The Easter version always contains *biała kiełbasa*, or "spicy white sausage," which is the same thing as bratwurst. Sometimes *żurek*, like its Italian cousin, *zuppa di pan cotto*, is served with hard-boiled egg. But it is always sour, salty, and creamy at the same time, which makes it unlike almost anything else.

Once you've tried it, the taste of *żurek* stays with you. Over the years Anne has encountered a number of Japanese who have been to Poland (there are more than you might imagine, such is the pull of Chopin's birthplace). Almost every single one of them specifically mentioned *żurek* as the one Polish food he or she would never forget. Perhaps there is some mystical link between sour bread soup and sushi; we leave that for others to interpret.

Our version is on the lighter side, and cheats somewhat by making a vegetable broth during the cooking process, instead of using plain water. We also like the spiciness of horseradish here and, perhaps for similar reasons, we prefer sausage to egg. Use Polish *biała kiełbasa* or bratwurst if you can get it, but if not, there are many lightly spiced chicken, veal, or pork sausages that would work here. They don't have to be precooked, as they will be boiled in the soup.

½ cup/115 g rye flour

1 or 2 crusts from rye bread (about 1 cup/225 g total)

2 garlic cloves, minced

2 cups/480 ml warm water

FOR THE SOUP

2 large onions, peeled, one halved and one coarsely chopped

1 large carrot, trimmed and peeled

1 large parsnip, trimmed and peeled

½ celery root, peeled

6 cups/1.4 L water

2 garlic cloves, chopped finely

¼ lb/115 g bacon (3 to 4 strips), chopped

2¼ lb/1 kg white sausage, cut into chunks

1 bay leaf

3 allspice berries

1 tbsp dried marjoram

6 black peppercorns

¼ cup/55 g grated white horseradish (jarred is fine)

½ cup/120 ml light cream

Crusty brown bread for serving (optional)

TO MAKE THE ZAKWAS: Place all of the ingredients in a large storage jar (a 1-qt/960-ml size will do) with a hermetically sealing top (such as you would use for preserving fruit). Leave the jar in a warm place—on a windowsill or in a cupboard—for 4 to 5 days. Open the jar, remove any mold or green bits that might have accumulated on top, and strain. The remaining sour, fermented liquid is the *zakwas*. You will have about 2 cups/480 ml for the soup. Set aside.

TO MAKE THE SOUP: Place the sliced onion halves, carrot, parsnip, and celery root in a large saucepan with the water. Bring to a boil, lower the heat, and simmer, uncovered, for 40 minutes or so. Strain the broth and discard the vegetables.

Meanwhile, in a soup pot, fry together the chopped onion, garlic, bacon, and sausage over medium-high heat until all are lightly browned. Add the strained vegetable broth, the bay leaf, allspice, marjoram, peppercorns, and horseradish. Bring to a boil, reduce the heat, and cook at a low boil for 20 minutes. Stir in the reserved *zakwas* and the cream. Raise the heat, and bring to a boil again. Remove the bay leaf and serve, preferably with crusty brown bread on the side.

Chicken Soup

ROSÓŁ

Serves 8 to 10

We don't know why it is that so many people so seldom make chicken soup from scratch. This is, after all, the ultimate comfort food. Though it might not really have all of the magical flu-curing properties attributed to it in both Polish and Jewish folklore, it is extremely healthful—the main ingredients, after all, are water and vegetables. It's certainly much healthier than the store-bought versions, which usually contain high levels of sodium and preservatives. A large pot can serve a dozen people; children eat it with gusto. The leftovers can last for several days, and can take many forms, the meat converted into chicken salad or chicken sandwiches, the broth used as a base for other soups. Chicken soup requires no culinary expertise, and it involves only the most humble ingredients. The actual preparation requires very little time: Though the soup does need to boil for a couple of hours, you needn't watch it while it does so. You can even turn it off halfway through cooking and then finish the boiling-down process later in the day, to no ill effect. We've done it many times.

For all of those reasons, chicken soup, or *rosół*, is the most basic, most beloved, and most frequently cooked dish in many Polish households. There are as many recipes as there are cooks. The one we are using here is most definitely for chicken soup, not chicken stock: The latter can be made with a handful of bones and leftovers, but the real thing requires actual meat, uncooked, if it is to have enough flavor to make a real meal. The trick to a really flavorful soup, in fact, is to use two kinds of meat—here we use chicken parts and a piece of beef on its bone—as well as more vegetables than you are usually instructed to use. (If you'd like a more delicately flavored chicken broth, you can omit the beef bone.)

Do feel free to add whatever you have in your garden or find at the market, remembering that some vegetables have quite strong tastes and can change the soup's flavor. Polish cooks sometimes put a slice of savoy cabbage into their *rosół*, and Anne occasionally tosses in a zucchini as well. Another popular Polish addition is lovage, an herb that was once very popular and featured in nineteenth-century cookbooks, but has gone out of fashion. It is sweetish, bearing a distant resemblance to fennel. Anne has it in her garden, and if you can find it—farmers' markets might have it in spring and summer—it adds an unexpected depth. Most Poles would draw the line at garlic: *rosół* is supposed to be rich but delicate, and garlic would overpower the rest of the soup.

continued

The only absolutely required vegetables are carrots, parsnips, onions, leeks, and celery root (though if you haven't got any of the latter, ordinary celery will do). In Polish markets you can buy these particular vegetables grouped together in bundles known as *wlosczyzny*, a word whose origins appear linked to the Polish word for Italy, which is Wloch. Allegedly, this is because Poland's Italian queen, Bona Sforza, brought soup vegetables to Poland from Italy (along with the tomato) in the sixteenth century. True or not, the name remains.

We call for 5 qt/4.7 L of water here, but if you haven't got a pot large enough, you can always add more water during the boiling-down process. Danielle reckons you need a seriously large chicken here, incidentally, and says that if yours is small, then use two.

5 to 6 lb/2.3 to 2.7 kg chicken, whole or cut up, bone-in (breasts, thighs, drumsticks, neck if you have it)

1 lb/455 g veal or beef on a bone (this can be shanks, ribs, anything cheap)

About 5 qt/4.7 L water (depending on the size of the pot you are using; there should be enough to cover chicken)

1 large onion, halved (no need to peel—the skin gives the soup a lovely color)

5 medium carrots, trimmed, peeled, and thickly sliced

2 large or 4 medium parsnips, trimmed, peeled, and thickly sliced

2 leeks (white and green parts), trimmed, halved lengthwise, and rinsed

½ head medium celery root, peeled and coarsely chopped, or 3 celery stalks, with leaves, coarsely chopped

1 slice savoy cabbage, or ½ zucchini (optional)

4 whole cloves

4 allspice berries

1 bay leaf

4 sprigs fresh flat-leaf parsley

4 sprigs fresh dill, plus a generous handful of chopped for garnish

1 thin slice lemon

1 tbsp sugar

1 tbsp salt

Handful of fresh lovage leaves (if you can get them; optional)

5 to 6 peppercorns

Salt and freshly ground pepper

Wash the chicken thoroughly. Put in large soup pot with the meat bones and add the water and onion. Bring to a boil, remove any foam that has risen to the top, and cook, uncovered, over medium heat for 30 minutes. Add all the remaining ingredients except for the salt and ground pepper. Cover and cook at a low boil until the meat is tender and the chicken is falling off the bone, about 2 to 2½ hours.

Remove the chicken and let rest in a colander set over a bowl to collect the drippings. Remove the meat bone and discard (or give to a deserving canine friend). With another large colander, strain the soup into a separate pot, bowl, or food storage container. (The latter is helpful if you are planning on refrigerating the soup overnight to allow the fat to harden, making it easier to skim. Many Poles don't bother with this, reckoning that the melted traces of chicken fat are precisely the magic ingredient that cures the flu). Press the vegetables against the colander to extract all their tasty juices.

Now here's where you decide which, if any, of the cooked vegetables appeal to you to serve in the final soup. Stop here if you want a clear, minimalist broth (if you are going to add matzoh balls or homemade noodles, for example). Skim the fat off the top (or refrigerate overnight and then skim, as noted above), and season with salt and pepper.

For a more robust meal, pick out the carrots, parsnips, and celery root from the colander. Slice these more or less elegantly and add to the skimmed broth (you can also add these after cooking the matzoh balls or noodles).

Now deal with the chicken. Remove to a carving board and pour the collected drippings into the broth. Shred the white and dark meat into more or less spoon-size pieces—your call as to whether you want to include the skin (a frugal Pole would, but neither of us finds it especially appetizing at this stage), and set aside. (If you're refrigerating the soup overnight, you can still go ahead and add the vegetables and shredded chicken. They won't interfere with the fat hardening. Or keep them separate in another container if you prefer, and add to the soup when reheating. Just don't add any noodles yet). You can refrigerate the soup for up to 1 week (in which case, skim off the hardened fat as directed and add the chicken and vegetables, if using, to the stock so they don't dry out. The soup can also be frozen at this point).

When ready to serve, reheat the soup and adjust the seasoning as necessary. Using a slotted spoon or ladle, distribute the chicken pieces and vegetables (if using) evenly and elegantly among the soup bowls, and ladle the hot broth on top. Garnish each with a sprinkling of chopped fresh dill.

Foolproof Matzoh Balls
KNEJDLACH
Serves 8

If you are making Chicken Soup (page 80) for Passover, then you'll need to make matzoh balls to go with it. For those who don't know, matzoh balls—*knejdlach* in Yiddish—are dumplings made from matzoh meal rather than flour. During Passover week, which commemorates their flight from Egypt, Jews eat nothing made with yeast. This is in honor of the Jews who fled from Pharaoh so quickly they had no time to let their bread rise.

The story behind this recipe goes back some twenty years. Danielle's mother-in-law, Barbara Frum, died just a month before Passover in 1992. The family was grieving, and it wasn't clear how that year's Seder would be pulled off. It was decided that each family member would provide a course, and Danielle was assigned chicken soup with matzoh balls. As a convert to Judaism, Danielle had not grown up learning how to prepare the holiday's traditional foods, let alone matzoh balls, which are famously difficult to make and can be notoriously disgusting. (Think hard, chewy pellets sunk at the bottom of an otherwise worthy broth.) An old family friend gave Danielle a recipe for chicken soup that her late mother-in-law loved (and that has been incorporated into our chicken soup recipe); but this friend wrote, at the bottom of the soup recipe, that she had despaired of ever finding a good recipe for matzoh balls.

Then, just before Passover, the food section of the *New York Times* published a recipe for matzoh balls that had been passed along through the family of renowned chef Wolfgang Puck. He served these matzoh balls at his famous Spago restaurant in Beverly Hills, as part of an annual Seder meal for his customers. Danielle made them that year: they were light, airy, and delicious. Her own family approved. The secret seems to lie in adding club soda to the mix.

6 large eggs
2½ tbsp finely chopped fresh flat-leaf parsley
1½ tbsp finely chopped fresh thyme
2 tsp sea salt
½ tsp freshly ground white pepper
Pinch of cayenne (optional)
½ cup/115 g clarified unsalted butter, melted
1½ cups/165 g matzoh meal
¼ tsp baking powder
1 cup/240 ml club soda
Chicken Soup (page 80)

Whisk the eggs in a large bowl. Whisk in the parsley, thyme, salt, pepper, and cayenne (if using). Whisk in the butter, and then the matzoh meal and baking powder. Finally whisk in the club soda until well combined. Cover with plastic wrap and refrigerate for 2 hours.

Bring the chicken soup to a boil. Whisk the matzoh ball mixture. With moistened hands, form into sixteen 2-in/5-cm balls. Drop the balls into the soup, reduce the heat so the soup simmers, and cook for 30 minutes. (You can do this in batches.)

Ladle the soup into bowls, place one or two matzoh balls in each, and serve immediately.

Dripped Noodles
LANE KLUSKI

Serves 6

Unlike packaged noodles, these noodles are made directly in the boiling soup, and are served immediately along with it. All noodle recipes of this kind call for eggs and flour, but in our view, the perfect proportions and most legible instructions are found in Hanna Szymanderska's *Polska Kuchnia Tradycjna*.

2 large eggs
1 tbsp water
Pinch of salt
Pinch of sugar
3 to 4 tbsp sifted all-purpose flour
Chicken Soup (page 80; see Note)

Crack both eggs into a small mixing bowl. Add the water, salt, and sugar and mix very well with a fork. Slowly add the flour bit by bit—you don't want to create lumps—mixing vigorously all the while. When the mixture is ready, it will resemble pancake batter and should be liquidy enough to drip slowly from a spoon.

Bring the chicken soup to a boil. Hold your bowl close to the boiling broth, and using a wooden spoon, slowly drizzle the batter into the soup so that it makes long, curly noodles. Using a fork, separate the noodles and let them boil for about 5 minutes. Remove the soup from the heat and serve immediately.

NOTE: *The soup yields more servings than this noodle recipe. Freeze a third or so of the soup for future use. Or make a double recipe of the noodles, which will work out fine.*

Next-Day Tomato Soup

ZUPA POMIDOROWA

Serves 4

This, as the name indicates, is the soup you make the day after you've made chicken soup, using the leftover broth. Like all recipes for leftovers, it is by definition inexact: Vary it according to how much broth you've got, how many people you want to feed, and so on. The recipe serves four people, but you can double it for eight if you have enough broth. This is a homey recipe, aspiring to nothing more than a role in a Sunday-night family dinner, alongside grilled cheese sandwiches or salad. Nevertheless, it is Anne's older son's favorite meal.

> 4 cups/960 ml chicken stock or leftover Chicken Soup (page 80)
> 2 large or 4 small fresh tomatoes
> One 14.5-oz/415-g can chopped tomatoes
> 1 medium onion, chopped
> Small handful of chopped fresh basil leaves (or, if you haven't got any, then chopped fresh dill, or if you haven't got that, 1 tbsp dried tarragon works, too)
> ¼ cup/60 ml light cream
> Salt and freshly ground pepper
> 1 cup/225 g cooked egg noodles, penne, or rice (optional)

Pour the stock into a large saucepan or soup pot over medium-high heat. While it is working up to a boil, remove the skins from the fresh tomatoes: Place them in a heat-proof bowl, cover with boiling water, and let sit for a minute. Drain and peel off the skins.

Cut the tomatoes in half, cut out the seeds and hard bits in the center, and chop roughly. Put in the by-now boiling stock and add the canned tomatoes, onion, and basil. Turn down the heat, and simmer for 15 to 20 minutes, until thickened.

Remove from the heat, and whizz the soup until very smooth with an immersion blender. Stir in the cream, season with salt and pepper, and reheat if necessary. Add the noodles (if using) and serve.

Mustard Soup

ZUPA MUSZTARDOWA

Serves 6

Anne met her friend Iwona Ciecierska on her very first trip to Poland, back in 1987, when Communism still thrived. Iwona had not yet launched her career as an architect and interior designer, and Anne still thought she wanted to be an art critic, not a journalist. Anne wound up sleeping on her floor. To this day her apartment remains, in Anne's imagination, the quintessential Central European city living space.

Iwona and her husband, Tomasz Ciecierski, one of Poland's best-known painters, live in the attic of a building in Warsaw's Old Town, with a loft for a bedroom, slanted ceilings, and tiny windows peering down onto cobblestone streets. The walls are covered with prints and paintings, mostly the work of Tomasz and their friends. The furniture is a mix of very contemporary and very old, and Iwona's cooking has an air of fusion about it, too: It is clearly Polish, but always contains an unexpected ingredient or a novel combination. She made this mustard seed soup for Anne and her husband for a late evening dinner after a concert (the Warsaw opera house is not far from her apartment). She denies inventing it—in fact, she told Anne that she first had a version of it in Holland, where Tomasz often goes to paint—but she has certainly given it her own twist.

Danielle once served this to guests with a few slices of smoked kielbasa sausage and croutons made from toasted black bread in each bowl. She figured it was like a deconstructed sandwich, elegantly presented. It was also very tasty.

For the mustard, you want the kind with seeds; smooth mustard will not work. And make sure you use a high-quality French brand, such as Maille, or the soup won't taste right.

2 tbsp unsalted butter

1 large onion, finely chopped

4 cups/960 ml chicken stock

1 jar (about 7 oz/200 g) whole-grain Dijon mustard

3 cups/720 ml heavy cream

Salt and freshly ground pepper

Handful of chopped fresh flat-leaf parsley

Melt the butter in a large pot over medium heat, and cook the onion until softened. Add the stock, raise the heat to high, and bring to a boil. Continue boiling for 5 minutes. Whisk in the whole jar of mustard, bring to a boil again, and then reduce the heat to medium. Cook at a low boil for another 15 to 20 minutes, stirring occasionally. Whisk in the cream and bring to a boil again. Season with salt and pepper. If the mustard flavor is too weak, continue to boil over medium heat until the soup is slightly reduced and the mustard taste is stronger. Stir in the fresh parsley just before serving.

When ladling into bowls, make sure to serve from the bottom of the pot, which is where the mustard seeds will have sunk.

Split Pea Soup

GROCHÓWKA

Serves 10 to 12

Grochówka automatically brings to mind the Polish army. Thus one's feelings about *grochówka* in Poland depend largely on one's feelings about the army, particularly if one has served as a conscript for a year or two, as all Polish men were once obliged to do. Nostalgia brings many back to this dish: Army field kitchens serving *grochówka*, bread rolls, and tea are often a feature of summer festivals, school fairs, and large public events in Poland. People happily eat a bowl or two, dished out by a soldier, and then go back to the merry-go-round for another ride. Anne's mother-in-law was horrified when Anne first fed it to her children: Was she preparing them for some future war?

In fact, this version of the soup is very child friendly, both smoky and sweet, and with a wonderful thick texture. The combination of thyme, tarragon, and good-quality meat removes any old institutional stigma as well. Nevertheless, this *grochówka* retains the advantages that led the army to rely on it in the first place: The longer it is cooked, the better it gets. It's worth making this in large quantities because it does keep for several days, and can also be frozen. But you can reduce the recipe by half if the army you are feeding is small.

1 lb/455 g dried green or yellow split peas

2 tbsp olive oil

2 leeks (white and green parts), trimmed, halved lengthwise, rinsed, and sliced into half-moons

2 medium onions, peeled

4 garlic cloves, chopped

4 large carrots, peeled, halved lengthwise, and sliced into half-moons

2 large parsnips, peeled, halved lengthwise, and sliced

½ celery root, peeled and diced

½ medium head savoy cabbage (⅓ if it is unusually large), any brown or wilted outer leaves removed, cored, and cut into strips

About ½ lb/225 g smoked Polish kielbasa, sliced

About ½ lb/225 g cured ham, cut into small chunks

1 tbsp dried thyme

1 tbsp dried tarragon

2 bay leaves

Salt and freshly ground pepper

Side salad and thickly sliced dark bread for serving (optional)

Place the peas in a large heat-proof bowl and cover with boiling water. Place a kitchen towel over the bowl and let sit overnight. If you can do this twice in the course of 24 hours, letting the peas cool and then straining and rinsing them in between soaks, so much the better.

In a large soup pot over medium-low heat, warm the olive oil and cook the leeks, onions, and garlic. After they start to get soft, add the other vegetables and cook for 5 minutes more. Add 4 cups/960 ml water, the sausage, ham, and peas, along with the herbs. Season with salt and pepper.

Bring to a boil, turn down the heat, and simmer, uncovered, for 2 to 3 hours; you want the peas to be soft, almost melted. Cover if you feel you are losing water too fast, or add a bit of water if it is too thick. You want the broth to be quite flavorful, not watery.

The boiling process does not have to take place all at once: on the contrary, the whole point of this soup is that it can cook almost indefinitely. You can, for example, start this after breakfast; bring the peas, vegetables, meat, and water to a boil, turn off the heat, and keep the soup covered on the stove top throughout the day. Then get another 2 hours of boiling in just before dinner.

Serve the soup as a meal in itself, or with a side salad and thick slices of dark bread.

CHAPTER THREE

Salads
and
Vegetables

Four Chopped Salads
CZTERY SURÓWKI
page 97

Celery Root and Green Apple Salad
page 98

Beet, Apple, and Horseradish Salad
page 99

Beet, Cherry, and Garlic Salad
page 100

Classic Coleslaw
SAŁATKA Z KAPUSTA
page 102

Butter Lettuce and Endive Salad
SAŁATKA Z SAŁATY I CYKORII
page 103

Grandpa Ben's Cucumber Salad
MIZERIA DZIADKA BENJAMINA
page 104

New Potato and Yellow Bean Salad
FASOLKA Z ZIEMNIAKAMI
page 106

Green or Yellow Beans à la Polonaise
FASOLKA SZPARAGOWA (ZIELONA
ALBO ZOLTA) À LA POLONAISE
page 108

Winter Roasted Beet Salad
ZIMOWA SURÓWKA Z BURAKAMI
page 110

Garlicky Carrots and Zucchini
CZOSNKOWA MARCHEWKA I
CUKINIA
page 111

Twice-Cooked Wild Mushrooms
GRZYBY
page 112

Red Cabbage with Cranberries
CZERWONA KAPUSTA Z ŻURAWINĄ
page 117

**Braised Cabbage with
Wine and Nutmeg**
WŁOSKA KAPUSTA W BIAŁYM WINIE
page 118

Roasted Pumpkin
PIECZONA DYNIA
page 119

Roasted Winter Vegetables
PIECZONA WARZYWA
page 120

Roasted Beets for Game
BURAKI DO PODANIA Z DZICZYZNĄ
page 122

Mashed Potatoes with Celery Root
ZIEMNIAKI Z SELEREM
page 123

Purée of Celery Root and Sunchokes
PURÉ SELERA Z TOPINAMBURAM
page 124

Celery Root Pâté
PASZTET Z SELERA
page 125

Four Chopped Salads

CZTERY SURÓWKI

The chopped salad might well be Central Europe's primary contribution to world cuisine. Mixed salads simply don't have as long a life here, because southern European salad vegetables don't have as long a growing season in Poland. In the past, lettuce wasn't available except for a month or two during the summer (though now, of course, it is flown in from Spain or Chile, just like to everywhere else). As a result, Polish cooks invented miraculous ways of combining root vegetables, fruit, and whatever else was in season, grating and cutting and splicing them altogether in unexpected ways. Poles call these cold salads *surówka*—which comes from the Polish word for "raw." It's customary to eat them all year-round, alongside your main meal. Room temperature *surówka* are eaten with hot meat and chicken dishes. The combination of hot and cold is deliberate, and often works well.

Four such salads follow. Two are based on beets, which are usually cooked first, before being chopped or grated. One is based on celery root. The final version is based on cabbage and is, of course, the dish that we Americans generally refer to as "coleslaw," though we hasten to add that it bears no resemblance to the sickly sweet dish, heavy with mayonnaise, that goes by that name in the United States.

continued

Celery Root and Green Apple Salad

Serves 4 to 6

This is a fresh-tasting side dish that would go well with chicken or fish. You could also set it on a buffet next to other chopped salads and cold meat.

1 celery root
2 Granny Smith apples
Juice of ½ lemon
1 tbsp olive oil
Salt and freshly ground pepper

Peel the celery root and cut into thin matchsticks. Peel the apples and cut into slightly thicker matchsticks. Toss together with the lemon juice and olive oil, and season with salt and pepper. Taste and adjust the seasoning if necessary. Keep chilled and covered until serving.

Beet, Apple, and Horseradish Salad

Serves 4 to 6

Beets and apples are often combined. Beets and horseradish are often combined, too. So why not try all three together? This is another classic set of sweet-and-sour Polish flavors.

5 large red beets
1 large tart apple
1 tbsp white horseradish (jarred is fine)
¼ cup/60 ml sour cream
Juice of ½ lemon
Salt and freshly ground pepper

Preheat the oven to 400°F/200°C/gas 6.

Wash and trim the beets and wrap them in foil. (Depending on the size of the beets, you can put three or four together in foil packages.) Place them in a shallow roasting pan and bake for 45 minutes to 1 hour, until they feel soft when pierced through the foil with a fork, but are still firm enough to be grated. Remove from the oven, open up the foil packets, and let cool. Slip off the skins (they should rub off easily) and grate the beets coarsely.

Put the beets in a large bowl. Peel and coarsely grate the apple and add to the beets. Mix together the horseradish, sour cream, and lemon juice in a small bowl and season with salt and pepper. Toss the beets and apples with the dressing. Keep chilled and covered until serving.

Beet, Cherry, and Garlic Salad

Serves 4 to 6

This recipe calls for sour cherries, which set off the sweetness of the beets perfectly. Sweet cherries can also be used here if sour are not available, although the taste is not the same. Fresh sour cherries are sometimes available in summer at farmers' markets, but it is possible to use frozen (defrosted) or canned sour cherries (drained) if fresh are not available. Anne has sour cherry trees in her garden, and she has happily used homemade cherry preserves for this salad in the winter. Like a chutney, it can be eaten alongside pork or chicken dishes all year-round.

²⁄₃ lb/310 g smallish red beets

FOR THE DRESSING
Zest and juice of ½ lemon
2 tsp grapeseed or other very light oil
¼ tsp dried thyme
¼ tsp dried tarragon
Salt and freshly ground pepper

⅓ lb/155 g sour cherries, halved and pitted
1 small red onion, finely diced
2 garlic cloves, finely chopped

Preheat the oven to 400°F/200°C/gas 6.

Wash and trim the beets and wrap them in foil. (Depending on the size of the beets, you can put three or four together in foil packages.) Place them in a shallow roasting pan and bake for 45 minutes to 1 hour, until they feel soft when pierced through the foil, but are still firm enough to be grated or sliced. Remove from the oven, open up the foil packets, and let cool. Slip off the skins (they should rub off easily). Cut the beets into thin strips, or else grate coarsely.

TO MAKE THE DRESSING: Mix all the dressing ingredients together in a small bowl.

Put the beets, cherries, onion, and garlic in a medium bowl and toss with the dressing. Serve at room temperature.

Classic Coleslaw
SAŁATKA Z KAPUSTA

Serves 4 to 6

This chopped salad makes a terrific summer side dish, and is perfect for picnics, whether you're celebrating the Third of May—the anniversary of the first Polish constitution, adopted in 1791—or the Fourth of July.

½ smallish head green cabbage (¼ if head is large)
1 tbsp sea salt
1 medium carrot, trimmed and peeled
1 tart apple, peeled
1 small onion, peeled
1 tbsp olive oil
¼ cup/60 ml plain yogurt
Juice of ½ lemon
Salt and freshly ground pepper

Core the cabbage and cut into long, narrow strips. Place these in a medium bowl, toss with the salt, cover, and leave for at least 1 hour. (Refrigerate if you are going to wait any longer than that.)

When ready to use, drain off any liquid. Cut the carrot and the apple into thin matchsticks and put in a large bowl. Coarsely grate the onion and add to the bowl. In a small bowl, whisk together the olive oil, yogurt, and lemon juice. Season with salt and pepper. Toss the cabbage mixture with the dressing, and taste to make sure you are happy with the seasoning. Serve.

Butter Lettuce and Endive Salad

SAŁATKA Z SAŁATY I CYKORII

Serves 4 to 6

What we call "butter" or "Boston lettuce," Poles would just call *sałata*—"lettuce." Butter lettuce—mild, slightly sweet, bright green—is the standard lettuce available in Polish markets and supermarkets. It's also what most people grow in their gardens. Iceberg lettuce, once the standard American lettuce, is a rare oddity. Poles haven't yet begun to buy plastic bags of prewashed designer lettuce either; most would harrumph at the ridiculous expense. So when they make a green salad, butter lettuce is what they invariably use.

The classic Polish salad dressing is white and creamy, made of sour cream, lemon, salt, and possibly dill. However, Anne has an aversion to creamy salad dressings of all kinds, possibly because she was made to eat bottled dressings as a child (much as her husband has an aversion to herring because he was once made to eat canned fish). Creamy dressings seem cloying, and they overpower the delicate taste of lettuce. The combination of the butter lettuce and the slightly bitter, crunchy taste of raw endive—sweet and bitter, pliable and crunchy—is perfect, particularly when tossed with raw garlic, olive oil, and salt. We always use sea salt with lettuce as the thicker grind is not absorbed by the leaves so quickly, and they are less likely to wilt.

Don't regard this unique, strong-tasting salad as an afterthought, something to be served, if you remember to, at the end of the meal; it can be elevated to the status of a main course side, right next to a mildly flavored piece of chicken or veal, or anything else that needs a bit of garlicky zing.

> **2 garlic cloves, crushed with a garlic press**
> **1 tbsp sea salt**
> **Freshly ground pepper**
> **¼ cup/60 ml olive oil**
> **1 large head butter lettuce, leaves separated, rinsed, and dried**
> **2 medium heads Belgian endive, trimmed, halved lengthwise and sliced crosswise into small white half-moons**

Combine the garlic, salt, and pepper to taste in the bottom of a salad bowl. Slowly whisk in the oil. Toss with the lettuce and endive, and serve.

Grandpa Ben's Cucumber Salad

MIZERIA DZIADKA BENJAMINA

Serves 4 to 6

Anne's grandfather was born in the United States, lived most of his life in Houston, and worked in the oil business. A lifelong Anglophile, he shared the enthusiasm of the British for tennis—he was a wonderful player—and for elegant shirts. He ordered his from Brooks Brothers, back when that was an unusual thing to do in Texas. Only recently did Anne learn that his family originally came from Odessa—another oil port, though on the Black Sea (in Ukraine) rather than on the Gulf of Mexico.

Perhaps this ancient genetic link to Eastern Europe explains the genius of this recipe, which he gave to Anne's mother. In fact it is a pitch-perfect *mizeria*, or Polish cucumber salad. Most Central European versions use cream, but we think cucumbers are more refreshing without it. Obviously, Anne's grandfather felt the same way.

> 2 large seedless English cucumbers
> 1 tsp sugar
> 1 tbsp chopped fresh dill, or 1 tsp dried dill
> 2 tbsp white wine vinegar
> 1 ice cube
> Salt and freshly ground pepper

Peel the cucumbers. Slice them as thinly as you can with a knife, or use a mandoline (the thinner and more translucent they are, the more elegant the salad). Put in a medium bowl and toss with the remaining ingredients including the ice cube. Allow the cucumbers to marinate in the refrigerator for about 1 hour. Taste, adjust with salt and pepper, if necessary, and serve.

New Potato and Yellow Bean Salad

FASOLKA Z ZIEMNIAKAMI

Serves 6

This is a recipe that passes itself off as a potato salad, but is in fact a celebration of the glories of fresh dill—the most popular Polish summer herb, and the one that just about everybody has in her garden. When it is at its height in July and August, we often stick a large bunch of fresh dill in a small vase with some water and leave it next to the kitchen sink, so the sprigs can be cut off and used anytime. This works out to just about every meal, from breakfast—it's great in scrambled eggs—onward.

Nevertheless, dill does go especially well with potatoes, and indeed, boiled potatoes are often served in Poland with dill and nothing else. This salad is a bit more elaborate than that, though not much. It is amazingly versatile, and can in fact be served hot (which is how our children like it) as well as cold. By adding small chunks of smoked ham, it also becomes the main course for a light family supper in the summer.

> 2 lb/910 g small yellow or white new potatoes,
> with their skins on, thickly sliced
>
> 1 lb/455 g yellow wax beans, trimmed
>
> Juice of 1 lemon
>
> 2 tbsp Dijon mustard
>
> 1 egg yolk
>
> Salt and freshly ground pepper
>
> 1/3 cup/75 ml olive oil
>
> 1 cup/40 g chopped fresh dill
>
> 1 cup/225 g diced smoked ham (optional; if you use sliced ham,
> the slices need to be thick, so the ham is chunky, not delicate)

Boil the potatoes in a saucepan filled with salted water to cover until soft but not too mushy, about 10 minutes. Drain and rinse under cold water. Boil the beans separately in salted water, about 5 minutes, until tender but not falling apart. Drain and rinse under cold water.

    In a salad bowl, whisk together the lemon juice, mustard, and egg yolk. Season with salt and pepper. Slowly dribble in the olive oil, whisking continuously until the mixture is emulsified. Toss the potatoes and beans in the dressing, add the dill and ham (if using) and toss again. Serve at room temperature.

Green or Yellow Beans à la Polonaise

FASOLKA SZPARAGOWA (ZIELONA ALBO ZOLTA) À LA POLONAISE

Serves 4 to 6

On French menus, the expression *à la polonaise* always means "with bread crumbs and butter," and sometimes "with parsley and eggs" as well. Fish, chicken, cauliflower, various other vegetables, and even eggs can be served *à la polonaise*. But in Poland, bread crumbs and butter have a special role in the preparation of green string beans and yellow wax beans—*fasolka szparagowa*—which can be bought by the bucketful in Polish markets when they are in season in July and August. Somehow the combination is perfect: The bread crumbs add crunch and the butter adds flavor to the mild-tasting beans, but they don't overwhelm either of these delicate vegetables.

Though this dish might seem, as the Poles would put it, *dziecinne prosto*, "childishly simple," this is a recipe that is easily spoiled, especially by those who overcook the beans. To get the proportions right, Anne made this dish with her friend Ola Klimont-Bodzinska, who has always served this to perfection (and who claims it is the ideal way to get children to eat their vegetables). They were making it for a large group—ten people for *obiad*, or "late lunch"—but the following recipe has been adapted for an ordinary family dinner. The most important thing, says Ola, is to use enough butter and bread crumbs so that they make a proper sauce, and not just a garnish. This recipe works best with younger beans, cooked until they are tender to the bite, without being soggy.

> 1 lb/455 g tender green or yellow beans
> Salt
> ½ cup/115 g unsalted butter
> 3 tbsp fine dry bread crumbs
> 3 tbsp finely chopped fresh dill
> Freshly ground pepper

Cut off the tips of the beans on both ends. (Don't cut them any further; the longer they are, the more elegant the presentation.) Fill a pot or saucepan large enough to hold all the beans with water, add 1 tsp salt, and bring to a boil.

When the water is boiling, place the beans in the pot. Return the water to a boil, turn the heat down to medium, and cook the beans at a low boil. Depending on the age of your beans, the size of your pot, and the strength of your heat, the beans should take between 10 and 20 minutes to cook. When you bite into them, they should not be crunchy, but neither should they be mushy. If anything, they are better slightly undercooked than overcooked. When they are done, remove them from the heat and drain well.

While the beans are cooking, melt the butter in a small saucepan over medium-low heat. When it begins to bubble, add the bread crumbs, spoonful by spoonful, stirring vigorously. With a wooden spoon or spatula, keep turning the mixture over until it turns golden brown and the butter is foaming slightly. Turn off the heat, pour the beans into a serving dish, and toss them with the bread sauce and the chopped dill. Season with more salt and pepper. Serve immediately.

Winter Roasted Beet Salad

ZIMOWA SURÓWKA Z BURAKAMI

Serves 4 to 6 as a side dish

We would happily serve this "salad" alongside a hot, wintery main course—a steaming dish of venison or a sizzling piece of fish. This is a vegetable dish that works either hot or at room temperature; somehow it doesn't matter.

3 to 4 medium red beets
¼ cup/60 ml olive oil
Heaping 1 tbsp Dijon mustard
1 tsp caraway seeds

Preheat the oven to 400°F/200°C/gas 6.

Trim the beets, but do not peel. Wrap each beet in tin foil (or in packages of two). Put in a shallow roasting pan, and bake until tender (pierced easily through the foil with a fork), approximately 40 minutes, depending on the size of the beets.

Unwrap the beets, and let cool just enough to handle (if you wish to serve them hot). Peel (the skin should easily rub off). Cut into thickish slices (about ⅛ in/3 mm).

Whisk the olive oil with the mustard and caraway seeds in a medium bowl. Toss the beet slices in the dressing and serve either hot or at room temperature, whichever you prefer.

Garlicky Carrots and Zucchini

CZOSNKOWA MARCHEWKA I CUKINIA

Serves 6 to 8

Marta Gessler, one of Poland's best-known chefs and cookery writers, once told Anne that when she is trying out a new chef, she asks her (or him) to make something out of carrots. If they produce anything resembling the chopped carrots and peas, drenched in mayonnaise, that were once ubiquitous in Communist-era cafeterias, she knows not to hire them.

Marta visited Chobielin once, and this is the carrot recipe Anne made for her—though to be honest, it isn't really a recipe. It's just an excellent way to prepare carrots and zucchini for a family meal—or a meal for friends—without drowning the vegetables in sauce. The numbers of carrots and zucchini here will depend on the size of the vegetables you have available: Roughly speaking, you want the same amount of each. This recipe is very easily doubled, or, for that matter, halved.

4 large or 6 medium carrots, peeled

2 medium zucchini

2 tbsp unsalted butter

2 tbsp olive oil

2 garlic cloves, roughly chopped

Salt and freshly ground pepper

½ cup/20 g loosely packed chopped fresh dill
(though you could, as Marta Gessler did later, make it
with thyme)

Halve the carrots lengthwise and cut them into sticks 3 to 4 in/7.5 cm to 10 cm long. Leave the skin on the zucchini and cut into sticks of the same size.

Melt the butter over medium-low heat in a large sauté pan, and then add the olive oil, followed by the garlic. Cook for 1 minute, and add the carrots. Cook for 3 to 5 minutes, until the carrots begin to soften, turning them over so that they cook evenly. Add the zucchini and cook, turning, until they, too, begin to soften, another 3 to 5 minutes. Cover the pan and cook on the lowest possible heat for about 10 minutes. Check occasionally to make sure the vegetables are not burning; add 1 tbsp water if they seem too dry. When they are done, they still should be slightly firm, but not crunchy. Sprinkle with salt and pepper, remove to a serving dish, and toss with the dill. Serve immediately.

Twice-Cooked Wild Mushrooms

GRZYBY

Serves 6 to 8 as a side dish

"Take me with you. I am very fond of picking mushrooms," he said, looking at Varenka;
"I think it's a very nice occupation."

When the serious, intellectual Sergei Ivanovich says those words to the shy, spinsterish Varenka during lunch at his brother Levin's country estate, the entire table understands what they mean: At last, Sergei will ask Varenka to marry him.

The mushroom-picking scene that follows is one of the most excruciatingly tense in the novel *Anna Karenina*, and indeed in all of Tolstoy's writings. Discreetly, the group leaves the couple alone in the forest. Both are aware that it is now or never. Varenka's cheeks are flushed; Sergei begins to practice the words of his proposal in his head. But at the last second, he puts a different question to her:

"What is the difference between the 'birch' mushroom and the 'white' mushroom?"

Varenka's lips quivered with emotion as she answered: "In the top part there is scarcely any difference, it's in the stalk."

The marriage proposal is never made.

Tolstoy's mushroom-gathering scene is one of several that feature in the literature of Central and Eastern Europe (another is in *Pan Tadeusz*, Adam Mickiewicz's epic poem of nineteenth-century Poland), and no wonder. Mushroom gathering is still, in many rural Polish communities, a central part of social life. After a late-summer or autumn rain, whole families go off into the woods to hunt mushrooms. In Communist Poland, factories and other workplaces would organize weekend mushroom-picking outings to the forest. These occasions were—as in *Anna Karenina*—famously conducive to romance. Poles who have immigrated to Britain or America are always amazed by the fabulous edible mushrooms that grow in public parks, which no one recognizes or seems willing to pick. Instead, we Anglo-Saxons prefer to purchase dried porcini at high prices in supermarkets.

During mushroom high season, between August and October, some Poles spend days gathering mushrooms, which they then sell in buckets by the side of the road. Nowadays, those who gather mushrooms, whether for love or for money, have increased their efficiency. One Polish website publishes a constantly updated Internet map, showing the best sites for particular mushrooms all over the country.

continued

As a result of all of this activity, wild mushrooms, whether fresh or dried, are a basic ingredient in traditional Polish cooking. They are made into sauces and soups, thrown into stews, and used to add flavor to pork and to game. Some would be familiar to a North American or European cook: *Borowiki*, the most prized Polish mushrooms, are from the boletus family, just like porcini. *Kurki*, which appear in late July or early August, are known outside of Poland as chanterelles. Others, such as soft *maszlaki* and the smaller *kozaki*—in English, "slippery jacks" and "scaber stalks"—have slightly different textures, the former being somewhat softer than the others, the latter crispier.

As for the following recipe, do be forewarned: Our method is not how Italians cook wild mushrooms, and it is not how a French person would cook wild mushrooms either. So if you are accustomed to crunchy porcini, lightly sautéed in oil, this recipe will seem odd. Don't let that put you off. The Italians and the French don't know everything about mushrooms, and this Polish version has a number of virtues. In Poland, wild mushrooms are often boiled twice, to remove dirt and soften, and are then cooked with cream. They come out meltingly soft, mild, and woodsy at the same time—perfect alongside other dishes, excellent when spread on toast, and superb by themselves, or perhaps over a couple of mashed potatoes.

> 1 lb/455 g mixed fresh wild mushrooms, cleaned and trimmed (see Note)
> 2 tbsp unsalted butter
> 1 small onion, peeled and minced
> ¼ cup/60 ml sour cream
> ¼ cup/10 g chopped fresh dill
> Salt and freshly ground pepper

Cut off the very bottom of each mushroom's stem. Chop the mushrooms roughly into chunks.

Put the mushrooms in a large pot and cover with water. Bring to a boil, remove from the heat, drain, and rinse. Cover with fresh water, bring to a boil a second time, and continue boiling for at least 20 minutes, until the mushroom caps and stems are completely soft. Drain the mushrooms, and strain the broth through cheesecloth if you would like to use it for another purpose.

Melt the butter in a large saucepan or sauté pan over medium heat. Add the minced onion, cook for 1 minute, and add the mushrooms. Cook for about 10 minutes, stirring occasionally, until the onion is translucent and the mushrooms are lightly browned. Add the sour cream and dill, stir well for another minute, sprinkle with salt and several good grinds of pepper, and serve immediately.

NOTE: *To clean wild mushrooms, use the edge of the blade of a paring knife to scrape off the thin outer layer of dirt, or use a soft vegetable brush. Mushrooms aren't usually washed as that makes them hard to dry, and they also deteriorate more quickly.*

To dry wild mushrooms, clean them and, with an ordinary sewing needle, pull a thread through the thickest part of each mushroom, both the stem and cap, until they are held together in a long chain. Hang the chain in a warm, dry place—somewhere near the stove is best. It takes about 3 weeks for the mushrooms to dry, depending on their size and the humidity. A less rustic and picturesque way to do this is in the oven: Slice the cleaned mushrooms very thinly (about ⅛ in/3 mm thick). Spread them out over a baking sheet in a single layer and bake at 150°F/65°C for about 2 hours, or until completely dry, turning once and blotting with paper towels to remove any liquid at the same time. Store in an air-tight container at room temperature. They will last for many months.

Red Cabbage with Cranberries

CZERWONA KAPUSTA Z ŻURAWINĄ

Serves 4 to 6

If green cabbage doesn't get enough respect, then red cabbage doesn't get enough attention. This is pretty much the only thing I ever serve with Venison Noisettes (page 179), but it would go equally well with duck breast (see page 164).

Leftovers can be used in the duck *pierogi* recipe (see page 211).

> 1 large head red cabbage
> 3 tbsp unsalted butter
> ½ cup/120 ml dry red wine
> ¾ cup/180 ml chicken stock
> ¼ tsp ground cloves
> 1 tbsp all-purpose flour
> ¼ cup/30 g dried cranberries
> Juice of ½ lemon
> Salt and freshly ground pepper

Core the cabbage and chop roughly.

In a large saucepan or Dutch oven, melt 1 tbsp of the butter over medium heat and cook the cabbage until softened, but do not brown (or it will become bitter). Add the wine, chicken stock, and cloves. Bring to a boil, lower the heat, and simmer, uncovered, for 30 minutes; the cabbage should be tender.

Melt the remaining 2 tbsp butter (you can do this in a small bowl in the microwave) and mix in the flour to create a paste. Stir it into the cabbage, add the cranberries, and continue to cook on low heat, stirring occasionally, for another 10 minutes, until everything is tender and thickened. Add the lemon juice and season with salt and pepper. Serve immediately.

VARIATION: *You can make this same recipe with fresh or frozen (and thawed) red currants instead of cranberries, though you will need to sprinkle in some sugar to taste when you add the currants.*

Braised Cabbage with Wine and Nutmeg

WŁOSKA KAPUSTA W BIAŁYM WINIE

Serves 4 to 6

Perhaps because it has so often been pickled in vinegar or boiled into limp submission, cabbage has acquired a bad reputation. But there are reasons it appears in so many European and Asian cuisines—cabbage is extremely hardy, grows in cold climates, and keeps its flavor and vitamins far longer than the more effervescent summer vegetables. It comes in different colors and shapes, and its leaves can be chopped, shredded, or carefully removed and used whole.

In Poland, cabbage is ubiquitous. In the days before refrigerators and imported produce, it was the only green thing available in the winter, and as a result, it has been incorporated into many different kinds of dishes, from plain and rustic to elegant and sophisticated. This recipe belongs to the latter category. Serve it on a dark winter evening, as a savory accompaniment to pork, veal, or game.

> 1 head savoy cabbage (though other kinds of green cabbage work here, too, including bok choy)
> 2 tbsp olive oil
> Salt and freshly ground pepper
> ½ cup/120 ml dry white wine
> Pinch of nutmeg, freshly grated if possible
> 1 tsp brown sugar

Core the cabbage and chop into shreds.

Warm the olive oil in a large skillet over medium heat, add the cabbage, and cook until soft, about 5 minutes. Do not let it brown, as it can become bitter (brownish is okay).

Season with salt and pepper, add the wine, and let it bubble for a couple of minutes. Turn the heat down, add the nutmeg and brown sugar, and stir. Simmer, covered, until tender, about 15 minutes. (If the cabbage is drying out or cooking too fast, add ¼ cup/60 ml water.) When ready, uncover and raise the heat to medium-high to reduce any extra liquid. Taste for seasoning and serve immediately.

Roasted Pumpkin

PIECZONA DYNIA

Serves 4 to 6

In Poland, pumpkins are generally eaten, not carved. Of course Anne carves them at Chobielin, since she is American. In the Polish countryside, this is a fairly eccentric thing to do, and the jack-o'-lanterns on her doorstep in October are the only ones around for many miles.

But if the Poles carve too few pumpkins, Americans *eat* too few pumpkins. Roast pumpkin is marginally messy to cook, but the result is spectacular: rich, savory, and colorful, and just the thing everyone wants to eat on a cold, gray day. It is quite common to add brown sugar to roast pumpkin, but unless you're serving children (in which case you might want to leave out the mace), we don't recommend adding it. Pumpkin is sweet enough on its own, and sugar can make it cloying. Serve this with pork or game, and light a jack-o'-lantern as a centerpiece if you've got one.

> 1 medium or 2 small pumpkins (between 10 and 20 lb/4.5 and 9 kg total)
> 1 tbsp olive oil
> 1 or 2 tbsp water
> 2 tbsp unsalted butter
> 1 tsp nutmeg, freshly grated if possible
> 1 tsp ground mace
> 1 tsp ground cinnamon
> Salt and freshly ground pepper

Preheat the oven to 325°F/165°C/gas 3.

Cut the pumpkin or pumpkins into manageable slices, depending on their size (usually this will be quarters). Scoop out all the seeds and stringy pulp (the tip or sides of a pointy soup spoon are usually good for doing this). Brush the olive oil over a baking sheet large enough to hold all of the pumpkin pieces, and then sprinkle the water over it; lay the pieces cut-side down. Bake for about 25 minutes, and then check the slices to make sure none is burning. Add more oil and water if necessary. Bake for about 20 minutes (the timing will depend on the thickness of the slices). The pumpkin should be soft, and the skin should easily peel off.

When cool enough to handle, remove the skin. Place the chunks of pumpkin in a bowl, and mash in the butter and spices. Taste after you're done with mashing—the texture should be somewhat lumpy. If there is any water—pumpkins give it off naturally—then drain. Season with salt and pepper, and serve immediately.

Roasted Winter Vegetables

PIECZONA WARZYWA

Serves 6 to 8

We like to think of this recipe for roasted winter vegetables as a kind of deconstructed chicken stock, without the chicken or water. The same vegetables are used here, but roasted instead of boiled. This is the time to take all your gnarly, ugly root vegetables, and turn them into a slick and elegant accompaniment to winter chicken, fish, or beef. The ingredients below are a suggestion—feel free to toss others into the mix.

Quantities will depend on how many people you've got to feed and how much space you have in your oven. The vegetables do have to be spread out, not overlapping too much, for this to work. We usually roast them on one or two rimmed baking sheets lined with foil, as it makes it easier to clean up afterward.

> **4 to 6 large carrots, peeled and cut on the diagonal into large pieces, maybe thirds or quarters (the way waiters cut bread in French restaurants)**
>
> **4 to 6 parsnips, peeled and cut on the diagonal into large pieces**
>
> **1 celery root, peeled, halved lengthwise, and thickly sliced**
>
> **3 to 4 small onions, peeled and quartered**
>
> **½ cup/120 ml olive oil, plus more if necessary**
>
> **½ cup/120 ml water or chicken broth, plus more if necessary**
>
> **Salt and freshly ground pepper**
>
> **½ cup/20 g chopped fresh flat-leaf parsley**

Preheat the oven to 350°F/180°C/gas 4.

Spread out the cut vegetables, in a single layer, on one or two rimmed baking sheets lined with foil. Pour first the oil, then the water evenly over them. Toss and shake the vegetables around, so that they are evenly covered in the oil and water mix. Sprinkle with a heavy dose of salt and pepper.

Place the baking sheets in the oven and roast the vegetables for 45 minutes. Then sprinkle with the parsley, mix the vegetables again, and add a bit more oil and water if any of them seem too dry. Roast for at least another 15 minutes, or until all the vegetables are soft and golden, but not mushy or burnt.

Toss again, add more salt and pepper if needed, and serve. This particular vegetable dish does not suffer from sitting in a low oven, so do make it in advance if you need to and then get on with cooking something else.

Roasted Beets for Game

BURAKI DO PODANIA Z DZICZYZNĄ

Serves 6

Like the potato, the beet is one of the most humble of Polish vegetables. Cheap and plentiful, and too often overcooked and oversweetened, beets have even acquired a bad reputation among some Poles. Until recently, the Polish foreign ministry didn't serve beets, on the grounds that they were too plebian to give diplomats. But beets have been rediscovered by upscale American and British restaurants, and so they've been "rediscovered" by Poles, too. Anne grows them in her garden, which means sometimes she eats them several times a week. She's tossed them in balsamic vinegar, cooked them in orange juice and ginger, mashed them into purées, and of course, made them into *barszcz* (beet soup).

But there are always other options. This gently creamy version, for example, goes beautifully with game—we would serve it together with the roast wild boar on page 193, for example.

> 2 lb/910 g red beets
> 2 cooking apples, such as Cortland or Granny Smith, peeled
> 2 tbsp unsalted butter
> Grated zest and juice of ½ lemon
> 1 tsp sugar
> 1 small piece fresh horseradish root, grated
> (or, if using jarred, start with 2 tbsp and add more if necessary)
> Large pinch of salt
> ½ cup/120 ml heavy cream

Preheat the oven to 350°F/180°C/gas 4.

Wash and trim the beets and wrap them in foil. (Depending on the size of the beets, you can put three or four together in foil packages.) Roast until just soft when pierced with a fork through the foil (do not overcook as you will need to grate them), about 1 hour, depending on the size of the beets. Let cool, unwrap, and remove the skins (they should rub off quite easily).

Coarsely grate the beets and peeled apples (you can use the grater attachment of a food processor for this), and toss together in a large bowl.

Melt the butter over medium heat in a large frying pan. Cook the beets and apples in the butter for 1 or 2 minutes, and add the lemon zest, sugar, horseradish, and salt. Cook for 4 to 5 minutes more. Stir in the cream and lemon juice until well mixed. Remove from the heat and serve immediately.

Mashed Potatoes with Celery Root

ZIEMNIAKI Z SELEREM

Serves 4 to 6

The potato is such a ubiquitous staple in Poland that, usually, little effort is expended upon it. Potatoes are peeled, boiled, salted, and then served alongside almost anything, really, and at all times of the year. They are also baked, fried, steamed, and puréed, or cut up and thrown into stews, just like they are everywhere else. But every once in a while one wants something different, and for those occasions we make this dish. It has the virtue of looking much like ordinary mashed potatoes, but tasting mysterious and unusual. If serving it to guests, ask them to guess the mystery ingredient.

> 2 lb/910 g baking or yellow potatoes, scrubbed clean, but not peeled, and cut into 1½-in/4-cm chunks
>
> 1 large or 2 small celery roots, peeled and cut into 1½-in/4-cm chunks
>
> Salt
>
> ¼ cup/60 ml milk, plus more if necessary
>
> 3 tbsp unsalted butter, plus more if necessary
>
> 1 tbsp minced fresh flat-leaf parsley
>
> Freshly ground pepper

Place the potatoes and celery root in a large pot filled with water, add 1½ tsp salt, and bring to a boil. When both vegetables are soft enough to be pierced easily with a fork, remove and drain. In the same (now dry) pot, or in a mixing bowl, if you prefer, add the milk, butter, and parsley to the vegetables, and sprinkle with salt and pepper. Mash together with a potato masher or with an electric hand mixer on low speed. The idea isn't to create a purée, but rather a rough-looking mash, with the skins in there, too, and little flecks of green parsley scattered throughout.

Add more butter or a few more drops of milk if the mixture looks too dry. Correct for seasoning and serve immediately.

Purée of Celery Root and Sunchokes

PURÉ SELERA Z TOPINAMBURAM

Serves 6

Celery root is one of the most humble and basic of vegetables. It grows in every Polish garden, and is an ingredient of almost every Polish soup. By contrast, sunchokes, also called "Jerusalem artichokes," are profoundly exotic. Anne has seen them for sale at Hala Mirowska, Warsaw's central farmers' market, but she concedes that there aren't many other places—so far—where they might be available.

And yet celery root and sunchokes have a natural affinity: both are root vegetables, both are ugly on the outside, both are creamy and smooth when cooked. Danielle spotted this essential similarity and decided to combine them when she was looking for something to serve with rack of venison (see page 180); this was the brilliant result. The taste is subtle and distinctive, and the consistency is deliberately thinner than a mash. It's something you would set the carved venison chops (or lamb rib chops, for that matter) in when serving, allowing it to puddle beneath the meat juices.

2 tbsp unsalted butter

1 large leek (white part only), halved lengthwise, rinsed, and chopped

1 large garlic clove, chopped

1 large celery root, peeled and cut into 1-in/2.5-cm chunks

4 large or 6 medium sunchokes, scrubbed, rinsed (you do not have to peel them), and cut into 1-in/2.5-cm chunks

2 cups/480 ml chicken broth

2 to 3 tbsp heavy cream

Salt and freshly ground pepper

In a large saucepan, melt the butter over medium heat and cook the leek and garlic just until the leek starts to sweat, about 3 minutes. Add the celery root and sunchokes and cook until lightly browned. Pour in the broth, raise the heat, and bring to a boil. Lower the heat, cover the pan, and simmer until the vegetables are soft, about 10 to 15 minutes. Let sit, covered, until ready to serve.

Rewarm the vegetables, if necessary, in their cooking liquid. Add a large dash of heavy cream. Using an immersion blender, blend the vegetables until smooth; they should be a little creamier and runnier than traditional mashed potatoes. If too thick, add a little more cream and blend again. Season with salt and pepper and serve immediately.

Celery Root Pâté

PASZTET Z SELERA

Serves 8 to 10

This is a recipe that you have to make to believe in. It doesn't sound like it will taste right, but somehow it does. The flavors of wild mushroom and celery root give it a woodsiness that make it seem almost like a game or meat pâté, even though it is completely vegetarian. Make it in a meat loaf pan, and then slice it like meat loaf as well. Serve the slices warm alongside chicken, beef, or pork, and save the leftovers to eat cold the next day.

The recipe comes from Anne's friend Bożena, who firmly states that all children love celery root pâté. She has five of them, so she should know. But she also wanted us to add a warning: When making this dish for people under the age of fourteen, leave out the nutmeg.

> 2 large celery roots, peeled
> 1 cup/240 ml olive oil
> 1 cup/240 ml water
> 2 mushroom stock cubes (available in specialty markets; or substitute chicken or vegetable stock cubes)
> 2 large onions, peeled and diced
> 4 large eggs, separated
> 1 cup/110 g fine dry bread crumbs
> 1 tsp ground nutmeg (optional)

Coarsely grate all of the celery root (you can use the grating attachment of a food processor if you prefer).

Combine the olive oil, water, and the stock cubes in a medium saucepan, and bring to a boil. Add the onion and celery root and simmer for about 1 hour, covered, on very low heat. Remove from the heat and let cool.

Preheat the oven to 400°F/200°C/gas 6.

In a small mixing bowl, beat the egg whites until frothy.

In a large mixing bowl, combine the cooked celery root mixture, the egg yolks, and the bread crumbs. Carefully stir in the beaten egg whites. If making the pâté for adults, add the nutmeg.

Pour the mixture into a nonstick or lightly greased 9-in/23-cm loaf pan and bake the pâté for about 1 hour and 15 minutes, until lightly browned on top and cooked through. A toothpick inserted in the center should come out slightly moist. Let cool a bit, then unmold on a platter. Slice thickly as if this were a cake, and serve.

CHAPTER FOUR

Main Courses

Trout with Lemon Cream Sauce
FILETY Z PSTRĄGA W SOSIE
CYTRYNOWYM
page 131

Sturgeon Steaks with Hot Mustard
JESIOTR Z SOSEM
MUSZTARDOWYM
page 132

Salmon Fillets with Caviar
FILETY Z ŁOSOSIA Z KAWIOREM
page 135

"Little Doves," or Cabbage Rolls
GOŁĄBKI
page 139

Cabbage Rolls with Wild Mushroom
Stuffing in Tomato Broth
page 140

Cabbage Rolls with Meat Stuffing
and Wild Mushroom Sauce
page 142

Chicken Breasts with
Chanterelle Sauce
KURCZAK W SOSIE KURKOWYM
page 145

Stuffed Chicken Breasts
with Cognac Sauce
PIERSÍ KURCZAKA Z FARSZEM
GRZYBOWYM
page 148

Chicken Salad with Arugula
SAŁATKA Z KURCZAKA Z RUKOLĄ
page 150

Chicken Blanquette Polonaise
GULASZ Z KURCZAKA
page 153

Weeknight Roast Chicken
KURCZAK PIECZONY PO POLSKU
page 156

Roast Chicken with Clementines
KURCZAK PIECZONY Z
KLEMENTYNKAMI
page 158

Chicken-in-a-Pot
POTRAWKA Z KURCZAKA
page 161

Duck Breast with Sautéed
Pears and Shallots
KACZKA Z GRUSZKAMI
page 164

Rich Turkey Patties in Madeira Sauce
with Potato-Chestnut Mash
KLOPSIKI Z INDYKA
page 166

Stewed Beef Rolls with Kasha
ZRAZY I KASZA GRZYCZANA
page 169

Kasha
page 171

Beef Tenderloin with
Wild Mushrooms and Dill Pickle
POLĘDWICA Z GRZYBAMI I
KISZONYMI OGÓRKAMI
page 172

Liver with Caramelized Onions
in Madeira Sauce
WĄTRÓBKA W MADERZE
page 174

Venison Three Ways
TRZY SPOSOBY NA SARNINĘ
page 176

Venison Noisettes
POLĘDWICZKI SARNIE
page 179

Rack of Venison with Prune Purée
COMBER SARNI Z SUSZONYMI ŚLIWKAMI
page 180

Venison Stew
GULASZ Z SARNINY
page 182

Hunter's Stew
BIGOS
page 184

Wiener Schnitzel, Polish Style
KOTLET SCHABOWY
page 188

Pork Loin Stuffed with Prunes
SCHAB PIECZONY ZE ŚLIWKAMI
page 190

**Roast Pork Tenderloin with
Orange and Rosemary**
POLĘDWICA WIEPRZOWA W
POMARAŃCZACH I ROZMARYNIE
page 192

**Roast Loin of Wild Boar
with Sour Cherries**
POLĘDWICA Z DZIKA Z WIŚNIAMI
page 193

Trout with Lemon Cream Sauce

FILETY Z PSTRĄGA W SOSIE CYTRYNOWYM

Serves 4

On the drive from Warsaw to Chobielin, there is a fish farm just before Toruń. The fish for sale are trout, the most popular and most common of Polish river fish. At the farm, the proprietor hauls the trout out of a tank; by the time they reach Chobielin, an hour or so later, they are still very fresh. When eaten right away, there is no more delicate a fish. After cleaning them, Anne wraps them in tin foil with some oil, salt, and herbs, and bakes them. With a few boiled new potatoes, it makes the perfect dinner for the first night in the country.

Since we don't think fresh whole trout should be eaten with a sauce, this recipe is for trout fillets. As an alternative to boiled new potatoes, Danielle suggests serving this with plain white rice, to which you have added 1 or 2 tbsp of butter and fresh parsley.

> **Fillets from 4 large trout, skin and bones removed**
> **About 2 tbsp olive oil**
> **Juice of 1 lemon**
> **Salt and freshly ground pepper**
> **2 tbsp unsalted butter**
> **1 large shallot, minced**
> **¼ cup/60 ml dry white wine or Vermouth**
> **½ cup/120 ml heavy cream**
> **Handful of fresh flat-leaf parsley, minced**

Place the fillets in a large flat dish that will hold them without overlapping. Drizzle with the olive oil and half of the lemon juice, turning the fish over to coat both sides. Sprinkle them generously with salt and pepper. Marinate for 30 minutes or so, flipping the fillets over once or twice.

Melt the butter in a large frying pan over medium-high heat. When it stops bubbling, brown the fillets quickly on both sides. Remove from the pan and set aside. Reduce the heat to medium and add the shallot to the pan; fry for a minute or two, until it has softened without browning. Add the wine and raise the heat to bring to a boil, scraping up all the bits of fish clinging to the pan. Add the cream and continue boiling until the sauce has reduced by about half and is thick and creamy.

Stir in the remaining lemon juice, reduce the heat to medium, and return the fillets to the pan. Cook, turning over once or twice in the sauce to ensure they are opaque throughout and warmed through. Garnish with the parsley and serve immediately.

Sturgeon Steaks with Hot Mustard

JESIOTR Z SOSEM MUSZTARDOWYM

Serves 6

Sturgeon has an exalted status in both Polish and Russian cooking, and no wonder: The fish is large and imposing, with the face of a catfish and the bony structure of a sea monster. Sturgeon are an ancient fish, and are thought to have evolved hardly at all for about 200 million years. But although the fish itself looks menacing, its meaty white flesh is extremely delicate, and it takes very well to sharp, lemony, vinegary, and mustardy sauces. For that reason, it graced the tables of the czars and Polish kings alike.

Polish sturgeon once swam in the Vistula, the river that runs through central Poland and was historically the main trading artery: Warsaw, Krakow, and Gdansk were all built alongside it. In more recent years, after sturgeon were fished out of the river, the sturgeon was brought from the Volga, where as we noted in our discussion of caviar (see page 42), it is also now endangered. But in very recent years, sturgeon farms have been created in more places than ever before—both in the United States and Europe—and sturgeon is now fished in the Great Lakes, and along the coasts of British Columbia and Northern California. As a result, it is usually available in specialty fish markets. If you don't have sturgeon in your local fish market, this sauce also works for trout, perch, and other freshwater fish with firm flesh.

If you do have access to sturgeon, the first thing you should do is ask the fishmonger to descale it and cut it into steaks.

> 6 to 8 sturgeon steaks, sliced about 1 in/2.5 cm thick (see Note)
> 1 carrot, peeled and roughly chopped
> 1 parsnip, peeled and roughly chopped
> ¼ celery root, peeled and roughly chopped
> 1 onion, peeled and roughly chopped
> 1 long sprig fresh dill
> 1 tbsp olive oil
> 1 tbsp white wine vinegar
> Salt and freshly ground pepper
> 1 lemon, thinly sliced into rounds, pits removed
> 3 tbsp unsalted butter
> 1 tbsp all-purpose flour
> 1 tbsp sharp English mustard
> Pinch of sugar

continued

Preheat the oven to 350°F/180°C/gas 4.

Place the steaks in a large, deep frying pan—the size will depend on the size of the steaks, but it should be large enough to hold all of them. Pour in just enough water to cover the fish, and bring to a boil. Continue boiling, uncovered, for 10 minutes. Remove from the heat. Carefully remove the steaks from the water with a slotted spoon, ensuring that they do not break, and place them on a plate.

Return the pan with the remaining water to high heat. Add the vegetables and dill sprig, and boil, uncovered, until the water is reduced by half. Strain the liquid through a fine-mesh strainer lined with a paper towel or cheesecloth. The resulting broth is your fish stock, which you will need to make the sauce. You will have approximately ¾ cup.

Place the steaks in a roasting pan large enough to hold all of the steaks. Mix together the olive oil and vinegar and rub this over the steaks. Season with salt and pepper.

Spoon a small amount of the broth over the steaks (just to moisten the tops and prevent them from burning). Place 1 lemon slice on each fish steak (about half the lemon slices). Bake for 20 minutes, or until cooked through.

Meanwhile, melt the butter in a frying pan and remove from the heat. Whisk in the flour until it makes a paste. Slowly whisk in the fish stock. Then add the mustard, remaining lemon slices, and sugar. Return to the heat and boil until thickened.

When ready, place the fish steaks on a serving platter. Pour some of the sauce over the fish and serve, passing around the rest in a small jug or sauceboat.

NOTE: *To prepare the sturgeon steaks yourself, you will need a very sharp knife and a bit of patience. Cut off the head and tail of the cleaned sturgeon and discard (or, better, use for the fish stock). Scrape the scales off the skin on the outside—you have to scrape very hard to make sure every bit of the scale is removed. Then cut the fish into horizontal slices, about 1 in/2.5 cm thick.*

Salmon Fillets with Caviar

FILETY Z ŁOSOSIA Z KAWIOREM

Serves 6

Red salmon roe caviar has never had the cachet of black caviar, but this is unfair—we suspect that it has lesser status simply because it is less expensive. It is often seen on Baltic, Polish, and Scandinavian menus, since both salmon and its eggs are native to the Baltic Sea. Anne has always had a secret fondness for red caviar, especially when served—as it logically should be—with salmon, one of the most popular fish in Poland.

Shiny, golden blobs of red caviar on top of smoked salmon on top of toast squares (or, as previously noted, on top of blinis) is a wonderful hors d'oeuvre. But red caviar on top of fresh salmon is even better. Anne invented this way of doing it one evening when she had some salmon steaks in her refrigerator and not much else—except a jar of red caviar, a gift from a Russian friend. The sauce is in fact a French beurre blanc, but it is somehow made more exotic and exciting with the addition of a dollop of caviar. This is an easy, quick recipe, yet suitable for the most elaborate dinner party or summer lunch. Anne has served it more than once on Christmas Eve instead of the traditional carp, simply because her husband likes it so much.

Danielle experimented with this dish, and declares that she wouldn't broil the fillets as Anne had been doing. She notes, "Since coming upon a recipe for roasting salmon in *Cook's Illustrated*, I have never looked back. Broiling can dry out a delicate fish, but roasting produces a foolproof, juicy fillet."

> 6 salmon fillets, preferably center-cut,
> all approximately the same size, with the skin left on
> 2 tbsp olive oil
> Salt and freshly ground pepper
> ½ cup/115 g finely chopped shallots
> 1½ cups/360 ml white wine, preferably dry vermouth
> 1 cup/225 g unsalted butter
> About ½ cup/115 g high-quality red salmon caviar

continued

Place an oven rack on the lowest position, place a baking sheet on the rack, and preheat the oven to 500°F/260°C/gas 10.

Rinse the salmon and pat dry. With a sharp knife, score the skin side of the fillets in several places, being careful not to pierce the meat.

Rub the salmon on both sides with the olive oil, and sprinkle with salt and pepper. Remove the baking sheet and reduce the oven temperature to 275°F/135°C/gas 1. Place the salmon skin-side down on the hot baking sheet and roast until the fillets are just cooked through, 9 to 13 minutes.

While the salmon is roasting, combine the shallots and wine in a large, deep frying pan and bring to a boil. Let the wine cook down to about ½ cup/120 ml. Continue cooking over high heat, stirring with a whisk, and add the butter, 1 to 2 tbsp at a time. Remove from the heat until the salmon is ready. Put the fillets in the sauce, and simmer for a minute or two. (The skin may come off in the roasting pan as you lift them—this is fine. Indeed, if you prefer the fillets without skin, remove it before placing them in the sauce.) Season with more salt and pepper.

Remove the salmon from the pan, put on a serving platter, spoon the sauce over the fillets, and spoon a generous 1 tbsp of red caviar on top of every piece. Serve immediately.

"Little Doves," or Cabbage Rolls

GOŁĄBKI

There is a reason why this dish is called *gołąbki* in Polish, which means "little doves." Although cabbage rolls can be too heavy and too filling, when they are made correctly they distinctly resemble delicate cabbage birds, nestled in a wild mushroom sauce or a simply enhanced broth. Like *zrazy* (stewed beef rolls; see page 169) or stuffed chicken breasts (see page 148), they are made with the humblest and simplest of ingredients, yet they are elegant enough for any reasonably festive occasion. When all twenty-seven European foreign ministers met for a celebratory dinner in a fabulous villa in the Old Town of Gdansk, the Polish hosts served tiny cabbage rolls, stuffed with buckwheat kasha, as a first course.

In truth, little doves are closely related to the stuffed grape leaves of Greece, and they ought to be thought of in the same way: A little bit of flavorful, spicy meat or mushrooms wrapped up in something green, with a light, creamy sauce drizzled on top. Serve the *gołąbki* with a side salad and you have a wonderfully healthful, comforting supper. Arrange them on a platter and you have an exotic appetizer for a dinner party or an addition to a buffet. Allow one or two stuffed cabbage leaves per person for an appetizer and three for a main course.

continued

Cabbage Rolls with Wild Mushroom Stuffing in Tomato Broth

Serves 6 as an appetizer, or 4 as a main course (makes 16 rolls)

2 large heads savoy cabbage

One 1-oz/30-g package dried mixed wild mushrooms or porcini

2 cups/480 ml boiling water

7 tbsp/100 g unsalted butter

2 tbsp minced onion

1 lb/455 g mixed fresh wild mushrooms, cleaned (see Note, page 115), trimmed, and coarsely chopped

⅔ cup/70 g dry bread crumbs

Salt and freshly ground pepper

2 medium plum tomatoes, sliced into thin rounds

1 tsp tomato paste

1 cup/225 g canned crushed tomatoes

Splash of chicken broth or white wine, if needed

Cooked rice for serving (optional)

Preheat the oven to 350°F/180°C/gas 4.

Fill a large pot—one in which you can submerse a whole head of cabbage—with water and bring to a boil. (It is helpful to use a pot with a strainer insert, such as a pasta pot, so you can pick up the insert to remove the cooked cabbage, rather than struggle with spoons or tongs.) Add the first head of cabbage and parboil for about 10 minutes. Remove and let it drain in a colander in the sink until just cool enough to handle. Meanwhile, cook the second head of cabbage, drain, and cool.

Gently pull the outer leaves off each cabbage. (Some of these might be soggy or torn.) Set these aside to line the baking dish. It helps to cut off some of the coarse stem at the beginning and while peeling off the leaves. Your goal is to have 12 to 16 perfect medium to large leaves in which to roll the stuffing. Set aside the small leaves for lining the baking dish as well. If you can get more than 16 leaves to stuff, do so—you can never have too many little doves. Pat each leaf dry and set aside on a kitchen or paper towel.

Soak the dried mushrooms in the boiling water for at least 30 minutes, until softened. Strain the soaking liquid through a fine-mesh strainer lined with a paper towel or cheesecloth, placed over a bowl. Set the liquid aside. Squeeze the mushrooms until the juices are all extracted. Rinse the mushrooms with cold water, pat dry, and coarsely chop.

Melt 2 tbsp of the butter in a large frying pan over medium heat, and cook the onion until translucent. Add the chopped fresh and dried mushrooms and continue to cook until all the mushrooms are soft and golden, 5 to 10 minutes, stirring often.

Pour the cooked mushroom mixture into a food processor and add the bread crumbs, a large pinch of salt, and a few grinds of pepper and process until well chopped and integrated, but not mushy.

Lay out the "choice" cabbage leaves on a work surface and divide the filling among the leaves: The exact portion size for each one will depend on the size of the leaf. (I dollop the filling on with a tablespoon, placing it near the bottom of the leaf). If any stem remaining on the leaf seems especially tough or thick, you can pare it down with a vegetable peeler. Roll the leaves up, folding in the sides and ends so the stuffing is enclosed.

Line the bottom of a 9-x-12-in/23-x-30.5-cm baking dish with any leftover cabbage leaves. (If, after lining the dish, you find you still have a lot of leftover leaves, store them in the refrigerator and eventually chop them, cook in butter, and season with salt and pepper to serve as a side dish for another meal!). Rest the rolls on top, seam-side down; they can be crowded together, just so long as they don't overlap. If you run out of room in one baking dish, start a smaller, second one, lining it the same way.

In a small saucepan, bring the reserved mushroom soaking liquid to a low boil. Whisk in the tomato paste and, when incorporated, the crushed tomatoes. Allow to boil for a minute or two, until slightly reduced and thickened. Pour over and around the cabbage rolls. The tomato broth should just come just up the sides of the rolls, but not submerge them. If there is not enough broth, top off with a little chicken broth or even dry white wine. Dot the cabbage rolls with 3 tbsp of the butter and layer the tomato rounds over the top. Bake for 40 minutes to 1 hour, or until the tops are golden and slightly crispy.

Remove the rolls to a warm platter, with the cooked tomato slices still on top. Pour the broth into a small saucepan, bring to a boil, and whisk in the remaining 2 tbsp butter. Reduce until the broth is slightly thickened and silky, and adjust the seasoning. Pour the sauce over the rolls and serve immediately.

Because these "little doves" do not have rice in them, they can be served along with a side of cooked rice for a more hearty meal.

Cabbage Rolls with Meat Stuffing and Wild Mushroom Sauce

Serves 6 as an appetizer, or 4 as a main course (makes 12 to 16 rolls)

FOR THE CABBAGE ROLLS

2 large heads savoy cabbage

5 tbsp/70 g unsalted butter

¼ cup/40 g coarsely chopped onion

4 cups/630 g cooked white rice

1 lb/455 g coarsely chopped boneless pork or chicken
(thigh meat will be juicier, but white meat works as well)

Salt and freshly ground pepper

2 cups/480 ml chicken broth or stock

FOR THE WILD MUSHROOM SAUCE

One 1-oz/30-g package dried mixed wild mushrooms or porcini

2 cups/480 ml boiling water

2 tbsp unsalted butter

2 tbsp minced onion

1 lb/455 g mixed fresh wild mushrooms, cleaned (see Note,
page 115), trimmed, and coarsely chopped (Go for an exotic mix,
but if your market offers only portobello, cremini, and shiitake,
these will work as well.)

1 tbsp all-purpose flour

Salt and freshly ground pepper

¼ cup/60 ml white wine, preferably dry vermouth

¼ cup/60 ml heavy cream

Juice of ½ lemon

Preheat the oven to 350°F/180°C/gas 4.

TO MAKE THE CABBAGE ROLLS: Fill a large pot—one in which you can submerse a whole head of cabbage—with water and bring to a boil. (It is helpful to use a pot with a strainer insert, such as a pasta pot, so you can pick up the insert to remove the cooked cabbage, rather than struggle with spoons or tongs.) Add the first head of cabbage and parboil for about 10 minutes. Remove and let it drain in a colander in the sink until just cool enough to handle. Meanwhile, cook the second head of cabbage, drain, and cool.

Gently pull the outer leaves off each cabbage. (Some of these might be soggy or torn.) Set these aside to line the baking dish. It helps to cut off some of the coarse stem at the beginning and while peeling off the leaves. Your goal is to have 12 to 16 perfect medium to large leaves in which to roll the stuffing. Set aside the small leaves for lining the baking dish as well. If you can get more than 16 leaves to stuff, do so—you can never have too many little doves. Pat each leaf dry and set aside on a kitchen or paper towel.

continued

In a small frying pan, melt 2 tbsp of the butter over medium heat, add the onion, and cook until lightly browned. Remove from the heat and put the onion, rice, and chopped meat into a food processor; season with salt and pepper; and whirl until well mixed. You want to be careful not to overprocess the filling—it should have the consistency of raw meatballs, and not be mushy.

Lay out the "choice" cabbage leaves on a work surface and divide the filling among the leaves: The exact portion size for each one will depend on the size of the leaf. (I dollop the filling on with a tablespoon, placing it near the bottom of the leaf). If any stem remaining on the leaf seems especially tough or thick, you can pare it down with a vegetable peeler. Roll the leaves up, folding in the sides and ends so the stuffing is enclosed.

Line the bottom of a 9-x-12-in/23-x-30.5-cm baking dish with any leftover cabbage leaves. (If, after lining the dish, you find you still have a lot of left-over leaves, store them in the refrigerator and eventually chop them, cook in butter, and season with salt and pepper to serve as a side dish for another meal!). Rest the rolls on top, seam-side down; they can be crowded together, just so long as they don't overlap. If you run out of room in one baking dish, start a smaller, second one, lining it the same way.

Pour in the chicken broth (it should come about a third of the way up the sides of the rolls, and not submerge them). Dot the tops of the rolls with the remaining 3 tbsp butter. Bake for 40 minutes to 1 hour, or until the tops are golden and slightly crispy.

Remove the cabbage rolls to a platter and keep warm (you can tent them with foil and keep them in the turned-off oven). Discard the leaves lining the baking dish, but reserve the broth, which will be added to the mushroom sauce.

TO MAKE THE WILD MUSHROOM SAUCE: Soak the dried mushrooms in the boiling water for at least 30 minutes, until softened. Strain the soaking liquid through a fine-mesh strainer lined with a paper towel or cheesecloth, placed over a bowl. Squeeze the mushrooms until the juices are all extracted. Set the liquid aside. Rinse the mushrooms with cold water, pat dry, and coarsely chop.

In a large frying pan, melt the butter over medium heat and cook the onion until translucent. Add the chopped fresh mushrooms and soaked dried mush-rooms, and cook, stirring often, until all the mushrooms are soft and golden.

Sprinkle the mushrooms with the flour, season with salt and pepper, and stir constantly until the mushrooms are well coated. Slowly add the reserved mushroom soaking liquid, continuing to stir until all the liquid is blended in and has thickened. Add the wine, cream, and any broth remaining in the pan in which the cabbage rolls were cooked, adding each one separately, stirring con-stantly, and allowing the sauce to thicken before adding the next. Add the lemon juice and lower the heat. Simmer the sauce for a good 15 minutes or so, until thick and rich. If the sauce is still too thin after 15 minutes, raise the heat and cook at a gentle boil, stirring, until reduced further.

When ready to serve, pour the mushroom sauce over the cabbage rolls, and serve immediately.

Chicken Breasts with Chanterelle Sauce

KURCZAK W SOSIE KURKOWYM

Serves 6

Chanterelles seem to have a universal appeal. When in season in Poland, between late July and early September, they are very cheap and extremely plentiful, and many Polish restaurants give over their entire menus to chanterelle worship, serving them in salads, sauces, and soups. The sauce in this recipe goes brilliantly with baked or sautéed chicken breasts, but it can be served equally well with pork cutlets, or as a vegetarian dish, spooned over boiled potatoes or pasta.

Anne has a particularly fond memory of eating a version of this sauce with boneless pork cutlets, lightly pounded and quickly sautéed. The chef was Julita Bodzinska, the mother of her friend Ola. Julita was serving the cutlets to the extended members of two families, who were gathered for a summer meal at her house, an old villa in the seaside city of Gdynia. She told everyone to help themselves to potatoes, then walked around the long table spooning large helpings of chanterelle sauce onto everyone's plates. After a while, she walked around once again, and spooned out more. Her youngest granddaughter, only seven years old, ate just as heartily as the older generation. It was proof, if any were needed, that everyone likes chanterelle sauce, regardless of age.

6 skinless boneless chicken breasts halves

5 tbsp/70 g unsalted butter

1 tbsp olive oil

3 medium onions, peeled and finely chopped

1 medium garlic clove, minced

⅔ lb/310 g fresh chanterelles, trimmed, cleaned (see Note, page 115), and chopped into small chunks

1 cup/240 ml chicken stock

1 cup/240 ml water

¾ cup/180 ml heavy cream

Salt and freshly ground pepper

continued

Preheat the oven to 350°F/180°C/gas 4.

Wash the chicken breasts and pat dry. In a large, deep frying pan over medium-high heat, melt 1 tbsp of the butter with the olive oil. When the butter stops foaming, add the chicken breasts and brown on each side (do not overcrowd the pan—you may have to do this in two batches). Remove to a shallow medium baking dish or roasting pan.

Add the remaining 4 tbsp/55 g butter to the frying pan. As it melts, scrape up any browned chicken bits with a spatula. Add the onions and garlic and cook over medium-low heat for about 5 minutes, or until the onions are translucent. Add the chanterelles. Reduce heat to low and continue to cook until the mushrooms are soft. Add the chicken stock and water and bring to a boil. Scrape any remaining bits of chicken from the bottom of the pan, turn down the heat, and simmer until the sauce has reduced and thickened somewhat.

Stir in the cream, season with salt and pepper, and pour the sauce over the chicken breasts in the baking dish. Bake for 15 to 20 minutes, until the chicken breasts are cooked through and the sauce is bubbly and lightly browned. Serve immediately.

Stuffed Chicken Breasts with Cognac Sauce

PIERSÍ KURCZAKA Z FARSZEM GRZYBOWYM

Serves 4

Poles will recognize this dish as an unusual version of *zrazy*, which are thin slices of beef rolled around various kinds of fillings, held together with toothpicks or skewers, sautéed, and then baked (see page 169). Quite a number of Polish recipes involve rolling and stuffing, and we think we see why: By applying a little bit of extra effort, you can, using quite ordinary ingredients, produce something that looks festive and unusual. Everyone likes to be presented with a dish, once in a while, that looks as if it took a bit of extra effort to prepare.

Because *zrazy* are often on the heavy side, Danielle experimented with the original idea, and has created a light version of this elegant dish. She used chicken breasts, which are easier to manipulate than beef, and filled them with wild mushrooms. The sauce is made with brandy, but while Cognac is lovely, there is no need to use anything very expensive.

2 cups/480 ml boiling water

1 oz/30 g dried *prawdziwki* mushrooms, or porcini if you don't have access to them, or other wild mushrooms, such as cèpes

2 tbsp unsalted butter

1 small onion, peeled and chopped

½ hard-boiled egg, peeled and finely chopped

Handful of finely chopped fresh flat-leaf parsley

1 tbsp dry bread crumbs

4 large skinless boneless chicken breast halves

1 tbsp olive oil

2 tbsp Cognac or another brandy

½ cup/120 ml sour cream

Salt and white pepper

Pour the boiling water over the dried mushrooms in a heat-proof bowl, and set aside for at least 30 minutes (you can also do this the day before and let sit). When ready to use, strain the soaking water through a fine-mesh strainer lined with a paper towel or cheesecloth and set aside. Rinse the mushrooms thoroughly, pat dry, and roughly chop. Set aside.

In a medium frying pan, melt 1 tbsp of the butter over medium-high heat. Add the onion, mushrooms, chopped egg, parsley (save a little for garnish), and bread crumbs. Sauté for a few minutes until the onion is soft, then remove from the heat. Transfer the ingredients to a food processor and whizz for one or two pulses—you want to have everything finely chopped, but not mashed. This is the stuffing.

Wash the chicken and pat dry. Using a very sharp knife, cut a 3-in/7.5-cm slit into the thick side—the long edge—of each chicken breast half and slide the knife in deeper to create a pocket. Divide the stuffing among the four pockets and seal the edges, using toothpicks or short metal skewers.

In a large, deep frying pan, melt the remaining 1 tbsp butter with the olive oil over medium-high heat. Cook the stuffed breasts briefly, approximately 2 minutes per side, until lightly browned. Remove from the pan. Raise the heat to high and pour in the mushroom water, allowing it to boil and scraping up any browned bits. Reduce the heat to medium-low, add the brandy, and whisk in the sour cream. Return the chicken breasts to the pan and simmer, uncovered, until the chicken is cooked and the sauce has thickened, 20 to 30 minutes. Season with salt and white pepper.

Remove the chicken to a platter, pour the sauce over, and garnish with the remaining parsley. Serve immediately.

Chicken Salad with Arugula

SAŁATKA Z KURCZAKA Z RUKOLĄ

Serves 6

The first time Anne ever served arugula in Poland—it was at a summer lunch party—some of the guests looked at her aghast. Arugula leaves bear an unfortunate resemblance to a weed that is quite common in that part of the world, and that's what they thought she was planning to give them. Since then, arugula has become as common as cabbage, and is even available in the supermarket in Anne's local town, Nakło. Though obviously not native to Poland, it grows beautifully there in the summer, not only in Anne's garden but anywhere.

Arugula also works perfectly in a main course salad with chicken, which, when cold, can otherwise be a touch bland. The arugula plays the same role that onions have in a traditional chicken salad, giving the meat an extra bite. What we love about this recipe is that instead of using heavy mayonnaise—which is what a more *echt* Polish recipe would do—it calls for a light mayonnaise dressing made out of a raw egg and some olive oil. This idea comes from a recipe for a similar salad, which Anne found in one of the Silver Palate cookbooks long ago, but she's made it so many times she almost never uses a recipe. It's absolutely the perfect main course for an alfresco lunch, alongside a couple of chopped vegetable salads. Serve fruit for dessert for the perfect light meal.

One note: This recipe calls for baking boneless chicken breasts, but you can use cooked chicken breast meat left over from chicken soup. Any other cold cooked chicken that you happen to have around is also fine.

> 2 to 3 lb/910 g to 1.4 kg skinless boneless chicken breasts
> Juice of 2 lemons, plus 1 tsp grated lemon zest
> ¼ cup/60 ml olive oil
> Salt and freshly ground pepper
> 2 tbsp Dijon mustard
> 2 tbsp white wine vinegar
> 1 large egg
> 3 to 4 cups/680 to 900 g arugula, rinsed, dried, and tough stems removed
> ½ cup/55 g sliced almonds, toasted

continued

Preheat the oven to 350°F/180°C/gas 4.

Place the chicken breasts in a shallow baking dish large enough for them to fit in one layer. Mix together half the lemon juice and half the olive oil, season with salt and pepper, and pour over the breasts, turning to coat. Marinate the chicken at room temperature for 30 minutes. When ready to cook, fill the baking dish with just enough water to cover the chicken breasts, place in the oven, and bake for 20 to 25 minutes, or until the chicken is cooked through.

Remove the chicken from the dish and let cool. Cut or shred with your fingers into long, thin chunks and place in a salad bowl.

Mix together the remainder of the lemon juice, the lemon zest, mustard, vinegar, and egg in a small bowl. Gradually whisk in the remaining olive oil so the dressing emulsifies. Season with salt and pepper.

Add the arugula and almonds to the chicken and toss with the dressing. Serve at room temperature.

Chicken Blanquette Polonaise

GULASZ Z KURCZAKA

Serves 4

French influence on Polish food is hardly surprising: Until recently, when English took over, most educated Poles spoke French. During the nineteenth century, when Poland was divided into thirds and occupied by the Russians (in the east), the Prussians (in the West), and the Austrians (in the south), Paris became the center of the exile community. French culture dominated life back home, too, as it did in most European capitals in an era when French was the language of diplomacy. Poland is also one of the few countries in Europe, outside of France itself, where Napoleon is still admired. Napoleon passed through Poland on his way to Moscow, and promised the Poles in the east independence from Russia, which he never delivered. Famously, he complained about the bad roads, some of which have still failed to improve.

This dish may well be something Napoleon left behind. There are many Polish variations of meat or poultry simmered in some sort of creamy mushroom sauce sprinkled with dill, and all of them bring to mind the classic French veal stew *blanquette de veau*. Danielle experimented with this dish, and decided to adapt the Polish version to the French one, substituting a cut-up whole chicken for the traditional veal shoulder and adding pan-roasted root vegetables to the sauce at the end (with, of course, mushrooms and a shower of fresh dill). The chicken is lighter, easier, and quicker to prepare than the veal, and the earthiness of the vegetables adds rustic depth to what is often a bland, rich sauce.

For a twist on texture, we used dried morels instead of ordinary mushrooms. If you prefer another type, go ahead—chanterelles or shiitakes would also work here—or, of course, use cultivated mushrooms instead.

continued

1 oz/30 g dried morels, or another dried wild mushroom of
your choice; or if you prefer, substitute ½ lb/225 g fresh brown
mushrooms (such as cremini) or white mushrooms, cleaned (see
Note, page 115) and trimmed

2 cups/480 ml boiling water

1 whole chicken (about 3½ to 4½ lb/1.6 to 2 kg), cut up into
8 serving pieces

Salt and freshly ground pepper

2 tbsp olive oil

3 tbsp all-purpose flour

1 cup/240 ml dry white wine

2 cups/480 ml chicken broth; plus 1 cup/240 ml chicken or
vegetable broth (optional; use if cooking fresh mushrooms)

2 tbsp unsalted butter, plus 1 cup/225 g

10 oz/280 g white pearl onions (We use the precooked frozen—
saves a lot of work. You do not need to thaw.)

1 large celery root, peeled and cut into 1-in/2.5-cm cubes

4 medium carrots, peeled and halved lengthwise

3 medium parsnips, peeled and halved lengthwise

1 cup/240 ml crème fraîche or light sour cream

Large handful of chopped fresh dill or parsley

Soak the dried mushrooms in the boiling water in a heat-proof bowl for at least
30 minutes.

Meanwhile, wash the chicken pieces and pat dry. Season all over with salt
and pepper.

Heat the olive oil in a medium Dutch oven or deep-sided, large frying pan
over medium-high heat. When the oil is hot, brown the chicken pieces nicely on
both sides. Do this in batches so as not to overcrowd. Set aside the browned pieces
on a platter. Return all the chicken pieces, with their accumulated juices, to the
pot and arrange in one layer. Sprinkle with the flour, tossing to coat the meat.

Raise the heat to high and add the wine. Let it bubble for a moment or so,
continuing to toss the meat, and pour in the 2 cups/480 ml chicken broth. Stir and
bring to a boil; immediately turn down the heat and cover the pot. Simmer the
chicken for about 25 minutes, or until all the pieces are cooked through, including
the dark meat.

Meanwhile, strain the mushroom soaking water through a fine-mesh
strainer lined with a paper towel or cheesecloth to remove the grit, and reserve
1 cup/240 ml. Rinse the mushrooms, pat dry, and chop.

Melt the 2 tbsp butter in another medium Dutch oven or large, deep-sided
frying pan over medium heat. Add the onions, celery root, carrots, parsnips,
and rehydrated mushrooms, tossing to coat. (Note: If you are using fresh mushrooms, cook them first in the butter until softened and light brown, then add the
other vegetables and proceed with the recipe.) Pour in the reserved mushroom
liquid (or substitute the 1 cup/240 ml chicken broth), cover, and reduce the heat

to medium-low. Simmer until the vegetables are tender and most of the liquid has evaporated, 15 to 20 minutes (the vegetables should be coated in sauce, but the mixture shouldn't be soupy).

Remove the chicken pieces from their pot when done. You should have approximately 2 cups/480 ml of liquid. Boil down the liquid until it is reduced somewhat to the consistency of a silky sauce. Lower the heat to medium and add the remaining 1 cup/225 g butter in chunks, whisking to incorporate. Remove from the heat and then whisk in the crème fraîche. Return the chicken pieces to the pot along with all the vegetables and their sauce. Toss until everything is well coated with the sauce, season with salt and pepper, and spoon onto a large platter or serving dish. Sprinkle with the fresh dill and serve immediately.

Weeknight Roast Chicken

KURCZAK PIECZONY PO POLSKU

Serves 2 to 3

Roasting a stuffed chicken on a busy weeknight seems like an ordeal, but in fact, nothing could be easier. The stuffing here is a classic Polish mix of bread crumbs mashed with fresh herbs and butter (as noted in the green bean recipe on page 108, a dish that is *à la polonaise* in French cooking is always made with bread crumbs and butter). Once stuffed, the bird can go in the oven, and you can mostly forget about it while you pour yourself a glass of wine and help your children with homework. In less than an hour you have an amazingly juicy, dill-infused bird that you can happily serve with just a simple tossed salad and a loaf of bread. If you're feeling ambitious, roast some vegetables alongside the chicken.

The stuffing does not amount to a side dish in the usual way. Instead, it makes a delicious herby crumble that melds into the pan juices, and turns into a kind of sauce. Danielle has made it with both store-bought dry bread crumbs and home-made fresh crumbs. The store-bought make for a slightly lighter, toastier version; the fresh absorb more of the juices, with a fluffier but more substantial result. Either is delicious.

To double the recipe, use two chickens and roast them side-by-side in the roasting pan. Using smaller, more tender organic chickens is important—don't go for the larger but less tasty roaster.

1 whole chicken (about 3½ lb/1.6 kg)
1 cup/110 g bread crumbs, fresh or store-bought dry
1 tbsp chopped fresh dill
1 tbsp chopped fresh flat-leaf parsley
½ cup/115 g unsalted butter, softened, plus 3 tbsp cold butter
Salt and freshly ground pepper
1 cup/240 ml white wine, preferably dry vermouth
Juice of ½ lemon

Preheat the oven to 350°F/180°C/gas 4.

Wash the chicken thoroughly, and pat dry inside and out.

In a medium bowl, combine the bread crumbs with the fresh herbs, and mash in enough of the softened butter so the stuffing holds together without crumbling. Season with salt and pepper.

Stuff the chicken and close the cavity with small metal skewers. Rub the outside of the chicken with any remaining softened butter. Place the chicken in a roasting pan.

Roast until the juices run clear when the leg is pierced with the tip of a knife, about 50 minutes for a 3½-lb/1.6-kg bird. Baste occasionally with pan juices to ensure a crispy, browned skin. Remove the bird to a cutting board and let sit while you prepare the sauce.

Skim off the fat from the pan juices and place the roasting pan over high heat until the juices bubble. Pour in the wine and bring to a boil, stirring constantly and scraping up the browned bits from the bottom. Add the lemon juice and the 3 tbsp cold butter and swirl into the pan. Cook until the juices are slightly thickened.

Carve the bird into slices or quarters, whatever you prefer. Spoon the stuffing onto the serving plate alongside the carved chicken. Pour over the pan juices and serve immediately.

Roast Chicken with Clementines

KURCZAK PIECZONY Z KLEMENTYNKAMI

Serves 4

This is our holiday version of weeknight roast chicken. Back in the days when clementines were a rarity, they were what you got in your Christmas stocking. Nowadays in Poland, as elsewhere, clementines are sold in cartons for the holidays, and Poles buy them in bulk, placing them in enormous bowls on the table and around the house, as an edible decoration and a symbol of seasonal abundance. Anne often puts them on a platter, sprinkles a handful of walnuts and some dates on top, and serves them with the after-dinner coffee, instead of dessert. That's all one wants after a heavy winter meal, after all.

Here the clementines are cooked whole, inside the chicken, where their juice sweetens the gravy and their zest gives it bite. This is a very easy dish, perfect for one of those nights around Christmas when you aren't entertaining hordes of cousins, but aren't in the mood for leftovers either. To add to the laziness factor, we throw some whole baking potatoes into the pan as well. Everyone loves this dish.

Again, as noted on page 156 in the recipe for Weeknight Roast Chicken, to double the recipe, roast two small chickens in the same pan, rather than roasting a larger one.

1 whole chicken (3 to 4 lb/1.4 to 1.8 kg)

1 tbsp olive oil

2 to 3 clementines, depending on the size of the chicken and the clementines (you will be using them as stuffing), peel left on

Baking potatoes, with skin on (optional; 1 per person)

Salt

1 cup/240 ml orange juice, preferably fresh-squeezed

1 tbsp chopped fresh rosemary, or 1½ tsp dried

2 small shallots, peeled and minced

Freshly ground pepper

continued

Preheat the oven to 350°F/180°C/gas 4.

Wash the chicken and pat dry. Rub the outside with olive oil. Stuff the whole, unpeeled clementines into the cavity—as many as will fit without spilling out. Put the chicken in a roasting pan.

Roast the chicken for about 1½ hours for a 4-lb/1.8-kg bird, or until the juices run clear when the leg is pierced with the tip of a knife, basting occasionally to brown the skin. For an even easier meal, rub some baking potatoes in salt, and place them in another roasting pan in the oven beneath the chicken—they will be ready when the chicken is. (Midway through roasting, pierce the potatoes with a fork in several places and turn.)

Remove the chicken to a carving board and let rest. Skim off any fat from the pan juices, and set the pan on top of the stove over low heat. Add the orange juice, rosemary, and shallots; raise the heat; and bring to a boil. Lower the heat again and simmer until reduced and thickened. Season with salt and pepper. You will want to have about 1 cup/240 ml of orange gravy.

Remove the clementines from the chicken cavity, cut them in half, and use them as garnish on the serving platter. Carve the chicken and pass the sauce separately. Halve the baking potatoes lengthwise and serve them alongside the chicken.

Chicken-in-a-Pot

POTRAWKA Z KURCZAKA

Serves 4 to 6

Danielle's husband, David, had a great-grandfather, Louis Hirschowitz, who ate the same meal for dinner every day throughout his adult life: boiled chicken with a potato and celery. He lived to be ninety-seven years old, kept every hair on his head, and retained all of his faculties to the very end. When it was occasionally suggested to him that he try to eat something different, he would reply, "If it was any good, I would have tried it already."

Once you make our version of this traditional Polish dish, you may be inclined to agree with Great-grandfather Hirschowitz, who was, of course, a Polish Jew. Whole chickens are boiled—or let's say poached, because it sounds better—with vegetables as if for chicken soup. But before the meat falls apart, it is rescued from the now delicious, rich broth. The rubbery skin is removed, and the pieces carved into elegant, juicy portions. These are served over rice cooked in the same broth, and dressed up with a very light, creamy sauce scented with lemon.

This is a wonderful recipe if you are feeling under the weather—more substantial than chicken soup, but with the same comforting effects. It also makes for a lovely weeknight casserole enjoyed equally by nostalgic adults and hungry children.

> 2 whole chickens (about 3½ lb/1.6 kg each)
> 2 medium carrots
> 1 medium parsnip
> 1 large onion, peeled and halved
> ½ large celery root, peeled and cut roughly in quarters
> 1 leek (white part only), halved and rinsed
> Handful of fresh flat-leaf parsley sprigs
> Freshly ground pepper
> 1 cup/215 g basmati rice (or the rice you prefer)
> 1 tbsp all-purpose flour
> 2 tbsp unsalted butter, softened
> Grated zest and juice of ½ lemon
> Salt
> 2 egg yolks

continued

Rinse the chickens and pat dry. Place in a soup pot or Dutch oven large enough to accommodate both chickens and the vegetables (we use a very big one, about 7 qt/6.6 L).

Trim the carrots and parsnip; you don't need to peel them (unless, like some, you wish to include these later in the casserole, in which case, do peel them). Cut each one into a few chunks. Add all the vegetables, along with the parsley and a few grinds of pepper, to the pot. Add just enough cold water to cover the chickens. Bring to a boil and then immediately turn down the heat. Cook the chicken and vegetables at a gentle simmer, uncovered, for about 1½ hours, or until the chicken feels tender when pierced with a fork, but is not yet falling apart. Remove to a platter and keep warm.

Strain the broth through a fine-mesh strainer into a large bowl, pressing on the vegetables to extract all their juices. Discard the vegetables (or, if you are keeping the carrots and parsnips for the casserole, chop these into bite-size pieces).

Skim the broth and use it to cook the rice in a medium saucepan according to the package directions (different types of rice will vary in their cooking times).

While the rice is cooking, carve the chicken into serving pieces (quarters or eighths, whatever you prefer, and remove the skin as you go, unless rubbery boiled skin is your thing). You can keep the bones in or separate them from the meat, also according to your own preference. You just want to keep the chicken in large pieces—not shredded or in chunks.

Skim and pour another 2 cups/480 ml of broth back into the now empty soup pot. (Any remaining broth can be frozen for future use.) Bring the broth to a boil, and reduce the heat to medium. Cream the flour and 1 tbsp of the butter together, and whisk into the broth so it thickens. Stir in the lemon zest and juice, and reduce the heat to a simmer. Return the chicken pieces (and vegetables if you are using them) to the pot and simmer gently for another 10 minutes or so. Add a healthy pinch of salt and a few grinds of pepper. Check the seasoning and add more if necessary.

When the rice is ready, spread out on a large serving platter and place the carved chicken pieces on top. Cream together the remaining 1 tbsp butter and the egg yolks, and whisk slowly into the sauce, bit by bit, so the eggs don't curdle, and the sauce is creamily thick.

Pour the sauce over the top of the assembled casserole (or drizzle a little of the sauce and pass separately) and serve immediately.

Duck Breast with Sautéed Pears and Shallots

KACZKA Z GRUSZKAMI

Serves 6 to 8

There is something very Central European about meat cooked with fruit. The Poles eat pork with apples, game with dates, and duck with almost any fruit. We've had duck *a l'orange*, of course (there is a Polish version, transplanted from France, that includes marjoram); duck with apples; and duck with plums. But on a recent trip to Budapest, Anne discovered an amazing recipe for duck with pears and shallots.

Hungary retains many links with Poland, both culturally and politically. There have been Hungarian kings of Poland, and Polish aristocrats in Hungary. At the time of the Hungarian anti-Communist revolution in 1956, the Poles staged an uprising as well. Some cynically point out that the two nations like one another so much precisely because they don't share a border, and thus have never had anything to fight about (unlike everyone else in Central Europe). But perhaps they share a similar palate as well.

This recipe comes from Anne's friend Noemi Koranyi, who says, "I did not invent it but I cannot trace the origins," which go back several generations. Try to imagine eating it on a snowy winter evening, as Anne did, at a table full of Hungarian intellectuals, all of whom are arguing about recent documentaries, history books, American foreign policy, and especially Hungarian politics, in multiple languages.

> 4 shallots
> 4 firm, ripe pears
> 4 duck breast halves
> 1 to 2 tbsp dried thyme
> 1 tsp fennel seeds
> ½ cup/120 ml pear brandy (this can be Poire William or the Hungarian version, pear *pálinka*)
> ½ cup/120 ml balsamic vinegar
> Salt and freshly ground pepper
> Fresh thyme sprigs for garnish

Position a rack in the upper third of the oven and preheat the oven to 425°F/ 220°C/gas 7.

Peel the shallots and thinly slice. Peel and core the pears and cut into small cubes.

Now contend with the duck. First peel off the skin, cut it into bite-size pieces, and fry the pieces in a frying pan over medium heat to make crispy crackling (they will generate enough fat to fry in—you don't need to add oil). Remove the cracklings with a slotted spoon and pat dry with paper towels. Leave 1 to 2 tbsp of rendered duck fat in the pan and remove the rest. (We save it for other purposes, including frying potatoes.)

While the skin is frying, rub the now-naked duck breast halves all over with the dried thyme and set aside. In the rendered fat, fry the shallots, pears, and fennel seeds over high heat until coated evenly with fat. Add the pear brandy and vinegar and cook, stirring often, for a few minutes, until the pears are soft. Season with salt and pepper. Remove from the heat but cover to keep warm while you cook the duck.

Place the duck breasts in a shallow, nonstick baking pan and bake for 5 to 6 minutes. The duck should be pink-rare—not raw-rare—in the center. Sprinkle with a little salt and pepper. Let sit for a few minutes, allowing the juices to settle. When ready to serve, cut the duck breast halves into thin slices. Place a dollop of the pear mixture on each plate and fan the slices over it. Garnish with the cracklings, and a few sprigs of fresh thyme.

Rich Turkey Patties in Madeira Sauce
with Potato-Chestnut Mash

KLOPSIKI Z INDYKA

Serves 6

The Polish ground beef patty—*klopsik*—is surely an ancient predecessor of the American hamburger (Hamburg itself being a northern German port that has traded with Poland for centuries). But unlike their modern American descendants, *klopsiki* do not rely on pure Texas beef for their flavor, and they are never served with buns. Instead, they contain spices and egg yolks, which help them hold together, and they are accompanied by a sauce—and, of course, boiled potatoes.

This version—all credit belongs to Danielle, who worked quite hard on it—eschews red meat in favor of lighter turkey, uses a Madeira sauce instead of the ordinary brown version, and replaces traditional boiled potatoes with a potato-chestnut mash. We've included two seasonal variations, one with culti-vated mushrooms, the other—just for fun, and only if you've got them—with fresh truffles. The two versions are meant to reflect the various possibilities of *klopsiki*: They can be homey weeknight food—children love them—or they can be dressed up for a special occasion. However you make them, the result is light, elegant, and autumnal, just like the grandmother of the hamburger ought to be.

FOR THE PATTIES

3 egg yolks

1 tbsp unsalted butter, softened, plus 4 tbsp/55 g, melted

2 lb/910 g ground turkey breast meat

⅛ tsp freshly grated ginger

Salt and freshly ground pepper

Juice of ½ lemon

FOR THE MADEIRA SAUCE

2 tbsp unsalted butter

1 tbsp all-purpose flour

½ cup/120 ml chicken broth, or more if needed

1 tsp soy sauce

¼ cup/60 ml Madeira

¼ tsp sugar (optional)

3 large baking potatoes, with skin on

4 cooked chestnuts (the precooked variety from a jar are fine)

4 tbsp unsalted butter, softened

Salt and freshly ground pepper

Dash of heavy cream

TO MAKE THE PATTIES: Preheat the oven to 375°F/190°C/gas 5.

In a large bowl, with an electric mixer at medium speed, cream together the egg yolks and softened butter. Add the ground turkey and ginger, season with salt and pepper, and mix together thoroughly, but gently, with your hands. Be careful not to overmix as you don't want to toughen the meat. Form the meat into small-ish but thick oval patties, about 3 tbsp of ground meat per patty. You should end up with about 12 patties, or 2 per person.

Pour the melted butter into a shallow bowl or dish into which you can dip the patties.

Heat a large frying pan over medium-high heat. When hot, begin dipping the patties, one by one, in the butter and fry until browned nicely on both sides (don't overcrowd the pan—you can do this in batches), pressing down gently on the patties for even browning. As they are done, transfer the browned patties to a roasting pan (into which all the patties must eventually fit without touching each other).

Bake the patties for 10 to 12 minutes, until cooked through (you can test by poking their centers with a fork—the juices should run clear). Remove the pan from the oven, squeeze lemon juice over the patties, and cover with foil to keep warm until the sauce and mash are finished.

TO MAKE THE MADEIRA SAUCE: Once the patties are in the oven, add the 2 tbsp butter to the now-empty frying pan over medium-high heat. Swirl the butter around as it melts, using a whisk or wooden spoon to scrape up the browned tur-key bits. When the butter foam subsides, quickly whisk in the flour, and when well mixed, pour in the broth and add the soy sauce. Continue stirring or whisk-ing until smooth, and reduce the heat to medium-low. Simmer the sauce and let it thicken for a few minutes. Add the Madeira and bring the sauce to a boil. Reduce the heat and allow the sauce to simmer while the turkey patties are roast-ing. Taste and add the sugar if you feel it would be nice to have the sauce slightly sweeter. If the sauce thickens too much, thin with a little broth.

continued

TO MAKE THE POTATO-CHESTNUT MASH: Cut the potatoes into quarters or sixths, depending on their size. Put in a medium saucepan, add water to cover and some salt, and boil until cooked through, 10 to 15 minutes. Drain and return the potatoes to the saucepan. (This can be done in advance of making the patties. When cooked, simply drain, cover, and keep warm.)

Add the chestnuts and mash together with the potatoes until well integrated (you can use a potato masher or, as we do, an electric or immersion blender). Add butter and season with salt and pepper, add the heavy cream, and mix until creamy smooth. Keep warm (not too long!) over a double boiler until ready to serve.

When the patties are cooked, place one or two atop a helping of mash on each plate, and finish with a spoonful or two of the sauce to serve.

TURKEY PATTIES WITH MUSHROOMS: *Add 4 small mushrooms (any variety), wiped clean (see Note, page 115) and finely chopped, to the ground turkey mix.*

LUXE TURKEY PATTIES WITH FRESH TRUFFLES: *Add 1 to 2 finely chopped small black or white fresh truffles to the ground turkey mix.*

Stewed Beef Rolls with Kasha

ZRAZY I KASZA GRZYCZANA

Serves 4 (makes 8 beef rolls)

Anyone of Polish heritage—or anyone who has been to Poland—will recognize this dish. *Zrazy*, or stewed beef rolls, are thin slices of beef rolled around various fillings. The rolls are bound with skewers, and are sautéed and then baked.

With its elegant presentation, *zrazy* enjoys a reputation for being *szlachetny* or "aristocratic." In Adam Mickiewicz's *Pan Tadeusz*, the saga of a minor noble family, and the greatest of all Romantic Polish epics, *zrazy* appear as the grand finale of a splendid late breakfast:

"W końcu wniesiono zrazy na ostatnie danie:
Takie bywało w domu Sędziego śniadanie."

"Finally they brought *zrazy* as the last dish:
That's what breakfast was like at the home of the judge."

Of course, since this is an epic poem, it rhymes in Polish.

Zrazy are served, in one form or another, all over Central and Eastern Europe. In Germany they are called *Rouladen*; they appear quite often in Lithuania and Ukraine as well and can be quite heavy. The key, as described below, is to use very thin slices of meat, and to pound them carefully, so that the beef serves to enhance the mushrooms and onions inside, and doesn't snuff out the other flavors altogether.

4 tbsp/55 g unsalted butter

2 medium onions, chopped

½ lb/225 g fresh mushrooms (any kind you prefer), cleaned (see Note, page 115), trimmed, and coarsely chopped

2 tbsp coarsely chopped fresh dill

2 tbsp fine dry bread crumbs

2 lb/910 g thick top round (London broil), sliced horizontally as thinly as possible by the butcher (⅛ to ¼ in/3 to 6 mm thick; see Note)

4 strips bacon, halved crosswise

Salt and freshly ground pepper

1 cup/240 ml dry red wine

1 cup/240 ml beef broth

2 tbsp cornstarch

Kasha (page 171) for serving

continued

In a large frying pan, melt 2 tbsp of the butter over medium heat, and cook the onions just until soft and translucent. Add two-thirds of the mushrooms and cook, stirring, until the mushrooms are softened and lightly browned, about 5 minutes. Transfer the onions and mushrooms to a food processor, add the dill and bread crumbs, and pulse until the mixture is finely chopped (but not mushy).

Pat the meat dry and flatten as evenly and as thinly as you can by pounding between sheets of wax paper with a meat pounder or the flat side of a heavy cleaver (or, our preference, the back of a heavy frying pan). Each piece of meat, once flattened, should be roughly 4 to 5 in/10 to 12 cm square. If they are long steaks, you can cut them in half.

Put a half strip of bacon on each steak. Spread about 1 tbsp of stuffing over the middle of the steak (you don't want to overdo it here, or the stuffing will leak out the sides of the roll). Season with salt and pepper, fold in the sides like two narrow sewing seams, about ¼ in/6 mm, and then roll up the beef. Tuck in the bottom, and secure with butcher twine. We find it best to tie up each roll like a parcel, with the twine running lengthwise and then crosswise, with a knot in the center. Trim any excess string.

In the same frying pan you used for the onions and mushrooms, melt the remaining 2 tbsp butter over medium-high heat. Brown the meat rolls on each side, in two batches. Remove them to a flameproof casserole or Dutch oven large enough to hold all the meat rolls snugly.

When all the rolls have been browned, turn up the heat under the frying pan to high and deglaze the pan with the red wine, letting it bubble and scraping up any browned bits on the bottom of the pan. Pour the wine and then the broth over the meat rolls. Sprinkle the remaining fresh mushrooms around the rolls, cover, and bring to a simmer. Cook for about 1 hour, or until the meat is very tender, turning the rolls occasionally so they don't dry out on top.

When done, remove the rolls to a platter and remove the string. Turn up the heat under the pot to medium-high. In a small bowl, whisk together the cornstarch and 2 tbsp of the warm sauce until smooth. Stir into the pot, and cook, stirring, until the sauce has reduced slightly and thickened. Pour over the rolls and serve immediately, with the kasha on the side.

NOTE: *You want the beef in long, wide pieces (8 to 10 in/20 to 25 cm in length), similar to veal scallopini, so they can eventually be rolled up.*

Kasha

Serves 4

If you are making *zrazy*, you have to make kasha to serve alongside. In fact, you might as well learn to make kasha anyway, because it is the perfect accompaniment to so many Polish dishes. Here is the traditional version, which may differ from the package directions.

> 1 large egg
> 1 cup/165 g kasha (roasted buckwheat groats)
> 2 cups/480 ml boiling water
> Salt and freshly ground pepper

Beat the egg lightly in a small bowl, add the kasha, and stir until well coated with egg. Pour into a heavy, medium saucepan over medium heat, and toast the kasha-egg mixture, stirring constantly, until the grains begin to separate. It should only take a couple of minutes. Add the boiling water, sprinkle with salt and pepper, and reduce the heat so the water simmers. Cover and cook for 10 to 12 minutes, until most of the water is absorbed. Turn off the heat and let stand for another 10 minutes or so. When ready to serve, give the kasha a good stir and check the seasoning. Serve immediately.

SERVING VARIATIONS: *This is a basic kasha recipe, but like wild rice, it can be combined with many things—toasted nuts, chopped fresh herbs, or sautéed mushrooms and onions. Feel free to experiment!*

Beef Tenderloin with Wild Mushrooms and Dill Pickle

POLĘDWICA Z GRZYBAMI I KISZONYMI OGÓRKAMI

Serves 6 to 8

At first glance, it may seem odd to pair the humble pickle with such a lofty cut of beef, but as with any good match, they end up complementing each other. Tenderloin can be bland and is too often served with an only slightly less bland wine sauce. But in this recipe, the pickles add a note of piquancy to the richly dense blanket of mushroom sauce; indeed, the whole dish reminds us of the forests surrounding Chobielin in late October—pungent, earthy, and fresh.

This is a wonderful early autumn dish, perfect for when fresh wild mushrooms are in season. If you don't have them in your local forest, look for a combination of wild species in a well-stocked market, such as chanterelles, shiitakes, porcini, oysters, and cèpes. Fresh homemade pickles, if you've got any (see the recipe on page 260), work wonderfully here. But equally good are any large size deli-style sour dill pickles, which Polish markets sell out of the barrel. And if you haven't got them, a good sour pickle from a jar works, too.

Serve this with wild rice and autumn vegetables, such as roasted pumpkin mash (see page 119) or roasted vegetables (see page 120), and a robust bottle of red wine. And do note that this recipe also works extremely well with pork medallions, provided they have been pounded and are sufficiently tender.

> 1 whole beef tenderloin (2 lb/910 g), cut crosswise into steaks, about ¾ in/2 cm thick
>
> 2 tbsp unsalted butter
>
> 1 medium onion, diced
>
> 1 large garlic clove, minced
>
> 2 medium sour dill pickles, diced
>
> ½ lb/225 g mixed fresh wild mushrooms (whatever is available at the market), cleaned (see Note, page 115), trimmed, and halved or quartered, depending on size
>
> Large pinch of sweet paprika
>
> Salt and freshly ground pepper
>
> ⅔ cup/165 ml dry red wine
>
> 2 cups/480 ml veal or beef stock
>
> ¼ cup/60 ml sour cream

Lay out the beef slices on a large sheet of wax paper. Cover with a second sheet of wax paper, and pound the slices gently with a meat pounder or the side of a heavy cleaver (or a heavy frying pan) until they are each about ¼ in/6 mm thick.

In a large, heavy frying pan that will hold all the beef slices, heat the butter over high heat until the foaming subsides. Sear the steaks quickly until browned on each side, 1 to 2 minutes per side. Do them in two or three batches if necessary. Do not overcrowd the pan, as the point is for them to be browned on the outside, but rare inside. Set aside on a platter or baking dish.

Reduce the heat to medium. Add the onion and garlic to the skillet and cook for a minute or so until softened, then add the pickles and mushrooms. Cook until the liquid given off by the mushrooms is of a thickish, syrupy consistency. Sprinkle with the paprika and season with salt and pepper. Add the red wine, stir, and keep the sauce at a moderate boil until reduced by half. Stir in the stock, return to a moderate boil, and reduce by half again. Lower the heat to medium-low, whisk in the sour cream, and keep whisking until the sauce is smooth and thickened.

Whisk in any juices that have collected around the resting meat, and return the slices to the frying pan. You can turn the heat up slightly to rewarm the steaks in the sauce. Turn them over once, and then spoon everything onto a large platter. Arrange nicely and serve immediately.

Liver with Caramelized Onions in Madeira Sauce

WĄTRÓBKA W MADERZE

Serves 4 to 6

Calf's liver (inexpensive, filled with vitamins) has the status of a miracle food in Poland and in many other places as well. Its role in Jewish cuisine—chopped liver in particular—is well-known to the point of cliché. We do realize that it has lost its health-food status in America because of its high cholesterol content, but we don't think eating it once in a while can hurt any more than the occasional dessert (and those vitamins are still in there). This dish is derived from one Anne tried at Restauracja 1921 in Bydgoszcz, the nearest big city to Chobielin. As its name indicates, this restaurant—part of the old Hotel Pod Orłem, the best in the city—serves the same dishes that were on the menu at the same restaurant in 1921, the year it opened. The chef cooks them in the same way, too, according to old recipes the restaurant still has in its files—calf's foot jelly, consommé, and tomatoes au gratin, among them.

The liver and onion recipe they use is very straightforward, though a touch of advance preparation is necessary. The only change we have made to the old-fashioned recipe is to cook the onions separately, and to caramelize them slightly, which adds a touch of luxury to this traditionally humble dish. When you are searing the liver, make sure that the pan is very hot, so that a crust forms on the outside and the inside remains pink and juicy.

1½ lb/680 g calf's liver, cut into even slices, about ½ in/12 mm thick

1 to 2 cups/240 to 480 ml whole milk

Salt and freshly ground pepper

¼ cup/30 g all-purpose flour

2 tbsp unsalted butter

2 tbsp cooking oil

3 large sweet onions, peeled and thinly sliced (Vidalia onions work best, if you have them.)

1 tbsp sugar

½ cup/120 ml Madeira

¼ cup/60 ml chicken stock

An hour before cooking, place the liver in a large bowl and pour in enough milk to cover. Cover with plastic wrap and leave in a cool place. When ready to cook, remove the liver from the milk and pat dry. Sprinkle with salt and pepper and dust with the flour. Shake off any excess.

In a large, deep frying pan, melt 1 tbsp of the butter with 1 tbsp of the cooking oil over medium heat. Add the onions, sugar, a few good grinds of pepper, and about 1 tsp salt. Cook the onions, stirring and tossing constantly to make sure they don't burn, until they are tender and brown, 5 to 10 minutes. Remove the onions to a warm serving dish.

Return the pan to the burner and raise the heat to medium-high. Add ½ tbsp of the remaining oil and ½ tbsp of the remaining butter. When the butter stops foaming, add half the liver, leaving some space between the slices. Sear for about 2 minutes on each side, keeping the pan hot enough to brown the meat, but not so hot as to burn the butter. As noted, the inside should still be pink, and when pricked with a fork, the juices should also be pink. Place the liver on the same dish as the onions. Repeat with the remaining ½ tbsp oil, ½ tbsp butter, and the rest of the liver.

Raise the heat to high, and add the Madeira and chicken stock to the pan, stirring and scraping the bottom of the pan to dislodge any leftover bits of liver or onion. Bring the Madeira and chicken stock to a boil, and boil rapidly until the sauce is reduced by at least half, and no longer runny. Return the liver and onions to the pan, turn over a few times in the sauce, and let them warm up for another minute. Serve immediately.

Venison Three Ways

TRZY SPOSOBY NA SARNINĘ

For far too long, venison has been considered a kind of backwoods dish, eaten only by men who like to get up before dawn and spend the early morning hours in a hunting blind. In Poland, hunting is controlled by hunting clubs, which tend to be all-male, often ex-army, and invariably observe multiple ancient rituals that involve alcohol and singing. But even Polish hunters are a more eclectic group than one would think. Klemens Sikorski, an uncle of Anne's husband, who collects and sells antiques and amber in a small shop in Mariacka Street in Gdansk, is a hunter. Anne's friend Rafał Jerzy, an animal lover with a house full of dogs and cats, and horses on the property, is also a hunter. A country neighbor Roman Barlik smokes eel, makes his own cherry brandy, and generally knows everything there is to know about organic food in Poland; he also owns a fabulous deer farm and is a hunter, too.

But you don't have to be a hunter to eat game. You don't even have to like hunting to eat game. Most of the venison that is eaten in Europe comes from deer farms, where the deer travel in packs and graze normally inside a large fenced-in property. They are carefully "harvested" once a year. Anne even contemplated starting a deer farm herself, and for about ten years, she actually kept a few fallow deer in an enclosure behind her house. She finally gave up, on the grounds that she just didn't have the acreage, but she did have a good supply of venison. There are many deer farms in Poland; and someone is certainly eating the venison they produce because Polish deer farms are profitable.

As a result of their activity, venison can now be found, frozen, in many Polish, British, German, and American supermarkets and farmers' markets, and venison is finally getting the recognition that it should have had all along. By definition organic, lean, and healthful—nobody stuffs deer with antibiotics, or feeds them ground-up fishmeal—venison is light, tasty, and low in fat. Because it has a strong flavor, it can be cooked with robust sauces and sharp spices. And since the taste of the meat improves after it has been frozen, it can be kept and transported with ease. The flavor often improves with long cooking times, too (tenderloin being the exception), which is why venison lends itself to stews and roasts—dishes that can be served to large groups of people. In older, prewar and nineteenth-century cookbooks, there is an enormous range of venison recipes from which to choose, which means that in an earlier era, plenty of people recognized the taste and value of this meat.

When cooking venison, there is one thing of which you must be aware: Venison needs to be marinated for as long as possible, and preferably overnight. The length of time is less crucial with a very delicate tenderloin, but when you are making a venison stew—and presumably using less elegant cuts of meat—you should count on marinating it for at least 24 hours.

continued

Venison Noisettes
POLĘDWICZKI SARNIE
Serves 6

These are made with the most elegant, most tender, and often the most easily purchased cut of venison, the tenderloin. This is the one cut of venison that does not have to be roasted, and is in fact cooked quickly, like filet mignon. When we make it, we use a white-wine marinade, which is less common than the red version but works better with a very lean, delicate cut of meat. We would serve this with Red Cabbage with Cranberries (page 117), a green salad, and nothing else.

> 1 whole tenderloin of venison (about 1½ to 2 lb/680 to 910 g), cut crosswise into steaks, about 1 to 1½ in/2.5 to 4 cm thick
> 1½ cups/360 ml olive oil
> ½ cup/120 ml white wine vinegar
> 6 juniper berries, crushed
> 2 bay leaves
> Salt and freshly ground pepper
> ½ cup/120 ml white wine, preferably dry vermouth
> ½ cup/120 ml Dijon mustard
> ½ cup/120 ml sour cream or crème fraîche

Wash the meat and pat dry. In a medium bowl, mix together the olive oil, vinegar, juniper berries, and bay leaves and season with salt and pepper. Pour into a large resealable plastic bag, add the steaks, and shake them around so they are covered in marinade. Refrigerate overnight.

When ready to cook, remove the steaks from the marinade and shake them off but do not dry them. Discard the marinade. In a large frying pan over medium-high heat, sear the steaks for maybe 2 to 3 minutes on each side, so they are brown on the outside but light pink on the inside. Set aside on a warm platter and tent with foil.

Reduce the heat to medium and pour in the white wine, allowing it to boil gently. Scrape up the browned bits of venison on the bottom of the pan, and add the mustard. Let it all bubble away for a few minutes more until reduced and thickened. Pour in any of the collected juices from the venison, and whisk in the sour cream. Return the steaks briefly to the pan, turn over in the sauce once, and spoon everything on the platter, arranging it nicely. Serve immediately.

Rack of Venison with Prune Purée
COMBER SARNI Z SUSZONYMI ŚLIWKAMI

Serves 6

Think of rack of venison as a meatier and more interesting alternative to rack of lamb. It also looks spectacular, if you are having dinner guests, or even if you just want to entertain your family. It is one of the few venison recipes that does not require advance marinating, and is best served rare to medium. Danielle likes it with Purée of Celery Root and Sunchokes (page 124), which she says is the perfect accompaniment because it doesn't overwhelm the flavor of the meat.

FOR THE PRUNE PURÉE
3 cups/680 g pitted prunes
2 cups/480 ml apple juice
1½ tbsp sherry vinegar
Pinch of salt

FOR THE VENISON AND SAUCE
One 8- to 12-rib rack of venison, halved to form two 4- to 6-rib racks (3 to 4 lb/1.4 to 1.8 kg total)
2 tbsp olive oil
Salt and freshly ground pepper
½ cup/120 ml beef broth
½ cup/120 ml cup red wine
½ cup/120 ml water
1 tbsp juniper berries, lightly crushed
2 tbsp unsalted butter

Preheat the oven to 425°F/220°C/gas 7.

TO MAKE THE PRUNE PURÉE: In a medium saucepan, bring the prunes and apple juice to a boil over high heat. Reduce the heat, cover, and simmer until the prunes are soft, 10 to 15 minutes. Add the sherry vinegar and salt. Using an immersion blender—or, if you prefer, a food processor—purée until smooth. The consistency should be slightly runnier than jam. (If too thick, add a few spoonfuls of warm water and blend again.)

TO MAKE THE VENISON AND SAUCE: Wash the venison racks and pat dry. Rub the racks all over with the olive oil and season with salt and pepper. Heat a roasting pan large enough to hold both racks over high heat until it is hot and sear the venison on all sides, in two batches if necessary. Arrange both racks in the pan (you can roast them side by side, standing up, with the ribs interlocked) and place the pan in the oven. Roast for 20 to 25 minutes for rare meat. Transfer the racks to a carving board and let sit, loosely tented with foil, while you make the sauce.

Heat the juices in the roasting pan over high heat. Add the broth, wine, water, and juniper berries and let the liquid bubble for a minute or so, scraping up any browned bits of venison from the bottom of the pan with a wooden spoon. Lower the heat and simmer for 5 minutes. Strain the mixture through a fine-mesh strainer, or a strainer lined with cheesecloth, into a small saucepan. Bring to a low boil over medium-high heat, and continue boiling for another 5 minutes or so to reduce until thickened into a silky sauce (it will resemble more of a *jus* than a gravy). Whisk in the butter and simmer for another minute. Season with salt and pepper, and remove from the heat.

Carve the venison into individual chops. Place 1 tbsp or so of the prune purée on each dinner plate, and fan two or three chops on top of the purée. Spoon 1 to 2 tbsp of the sauce over each portion. Serve immediately.

Venison Stew
GULASZ Z SARNINY
Serves 8 to 10

This stew recipe is designed specifically to soften tougher cuts of meat; we recommend the shoulder. The recipe calls for an overnight marinade, and will need to cook for a couple of hours as well. The addition of dates, fennel, and Madeira gives the meat a sweet flavor, which combines beautifully with pungent cloves and allspice berries. This is an excellent winter meal, but because of the heavenly aromas, it is a good thing to eat in the fall or early spring as well. We like to serve the stew with Mashed Potatoes with Celery Root (page 123).

FOR THE MARINADE

6 cups/1.4 L dry red wine

½ cup/120 ml red wine vinegar

1 cup/240 ml sweet port or Madeira

6 juniper berries, lightly crushed

3 whole cloves

3 allspice berries, lightly crushed

1 large head garlic, cloves peeled and crushed

Salt and freshly ground pepper

3 lb/1.4 kg venison shoulder, trimmed of fat and cut into 2-in/5-cm cubes

2 tbsp olive oil

3 strips bacon, chopped into 1-in-/2.5-cm-long pieces

2 large fennel bulbs, trimmed and thickly sliced

1 cup/150 g chopped dates

2 large onions, peeled and thinly sliced

1 tsp sugar

Salt and freshly ground pepper

TO MAKE THE MARINADE: Combine all the marinade ingredients in a large bowl.

Rinse the meat and pat dry. Place the meat in the bowl with the marinade, toss to coat, cover with plastic wrap, and refrigerate overnight or longer. (You can marinate venison for up to 3 days—it never hurts.)

When ready to cook, preheat the oven to 350°F/180°C/gas 4. Remove the venison pieces from the marinade and pat dry. Reserve the marinade.

In a large Dutch oven or stew pot, heat the olive oil over medium-high heat. Fry the bacon for a minute or two, until just crisp. Remove the bacon and set aside on a paper towel, leaving the fat in the pot. Raise the heat to high, add the venison, and brown well on all sides (do not overcrowd the meat—do this in two or three batches). Remove the meat and set aside. Pour the marinade into the pot, and bring to a boil, scraping up the browned bits on the bottom with a wooden spoon. Return the bacon and meat to the pot, and stir so they're well mixed with the liquid. Cover immediately and place in the preheated oven.

After 1 hour, remove the pot from the oven and stir in the fennel, dates, onions, and sugar. Taste the broth and season with salt and pepper. Return the pot to the oven and cook, uncovered, for another 45 minutes.

Remove from the oven and serve immediately, or let cool, refrigerate, and reheat later. This will last for several days, refrigerated.

Hunter's Stew

BIGOS

Serves 8 to 10

Bigos is one of the most widely eaten and beloved of Polish meals, and there are as many recipes for it as there are cooks. Though nowadays it is often made with only pork, it is not only more culturally accurate but more beguiling if you can add venison, as well as beef or veal and a couple of different kinds of dried Polish sausage. Poultry is never used in *bigos*, but any kind of dark meat or game is fine. The greater the variety of meats you use, the better it tastes. So do experiment.

Bigos is very hearty, and is usually served as a single course, always with thick slices of bread, and sometimes with a green salad. Because it is a one-pot meal containing both meat and vegetables, it functions much the same way as chili does in the United States. *Bigos* is served at large family gatherings, big outdoor events, potlucks, and picnics. Not surprisingly, given the tradition of cooking it with game, it's the thing you serve after a day's hunting. If you are roasting sausages around a bonfire, you might serve *bigos* alongside. If you are having a New Year's Eve party, you might serve *bigos* just after midnight, to keep the dancing going. *Bigos* was often served this way at Polish country house balls in the past, long after dinner had been consumed. (Alternatively, you may decide—as Anne once did at the end of a New Year's Eve party—not to serve the *bigos* because everyone is having too much fun dancing. In that case, one can eat it for lunch the following day).

This combination of ingredients will be unfamiliar to American cooks, but that shouldn't dissuade you. We promise that the slightly sour, spicy result will be delicious—and an exotic change from more familiar stews. Do feel free to double or triple the recipe; Poles often do.

continued

1¾ lb/800 g sauerkraut

4 strips bacon or, even better, 4 thin slices Canadian bacon, diced

1 small head green cabbage, thinly sliced

Small handful of dried wild mushrooms (any kind)

½ lb/225 g boneless venison, leg, or a stewing cut (not the loin), cut into 1-in/2.5-cm pieces (slightly smaller than your usual stew size; see Note)

½ lb/225 g boneless stew beef, such as chuck, cut into 1-in/2.5-cm pieces

½ lb/225 g pork or veal shoulder, cut into 1-in/2.5-cm pieces

¼ cup/30 g all-purpose flour

3 tbsp vegetable oil or lard

1 medium onion, peeled and chopped

1 cup/240 ml dry red wine

½ lb/225 g smoked kielbasa or another spicy hard sausage, thickly sliced

1 cup/225 g pitted prunes, quartered

Salt and freshly ground pepper

Bread for serving, preferably rustic and dark, such as a Russian loaf

Drain the sauerkraut, place it in a medium saucepan, and add 2 cups/480 ml water and bacon pieces. Cover and boil over medium heat for 20 minutes or longer, until the sauerkraut is very tender and the bacon is cooked. Meanwhile, put the fresh cabbage and dried mushrooms in a separate large saucepan, cover with water, and bring to a boil. Continue boiling until the cabbage is tender, 20 to 30 minutes. Drain and set aside.

Rinse all the meat and pat dry. Put the flour in a shallow bowl and toss the meat to coat.

Heat 1 tbsp of the vegetable oil over medium heat in a stew pot large enough to hold all the meat and vegetables. Cook the onion until softened, remove with a slotted spoon, and set aside. Add the remaining 2 tbsp oil to the pot and lightly brown the meat, in batches, over medium heat, 2 to 3 minutes per side, transferring the meat to a plate when it's done. When all the meat has been browned, raise the heat to high, pour in the wine, and boil briefly, scraping up the browned bits on the bottom of the pot with a wooden spoon. Return the meat and all its resting juices back to the pot, and add the onion, kielbasa, prunes, and the sauerkraut and bacon mixture, along with its cooking water. Salt generously, add several grinds of pepper, and bring to a boil.

Turn down the heat, cover the pot with the lid slightly askew, and simmer on very low heat for a good 2 to 3 hours, until the meat falls apart and the broth is rich and brown. Stir the stew occasionally, and ensure that the liquid isn't evaporating too quickly (add a small amount of water when necessary). Some like a watery *bigos*, but we find the tastiest outcome is for the sauerkraut, cabbage, and meat all to be practically melted together, with enough sauce to keep everything moist, but not so much that any of the ingredients float, as in a more traditional stew.

Serve in a large casserole with a big spoon and thick slices of dark peasant bread. You'll of course need utensils, but the fun of it is to shovel the *bigos* and its juices on to the bread.

Bigos lasts forever, and gets better with time. One of Anne's friends routinely makes this on Wednesday to serve on Saturday night, and swears that it improves every day.

NOTE: *You want 1½ lb/680 g meat altogether. If you can't get venison, use a combination of beef and pork or veal.*

Wiener Schnitzel, Polish Style

KOTLET SCHABOWY

Serves 4 to 6

Kotlet schabowy is what Anne calls, in her house, "kid food," and what the British call "nursery food." The Poles would call it "Sunday dinner," since it is probably the meal most commonly made in Polish households for large groups of people, especially when many of them are family members and some of them are children. When Anne had to feed five teenage boys on a recent weekend, she made *kotlet schabowy*. When her children go to a restaurant and see *kotlet schabowy* on the menu, they sigh with relief and snap the menu shut, and her husband likes to order it sometimes, too.

The dish is closely related to what German speakers call *Wiener Schnitzel*, though the *echt* Austrian version is made with veal cutlets and not pork. In both the German and Slavic worlds, this is what students would order in a pub, together with a glass of beer and some dill pickles, and what groups of skiers would eat on top of an Alpine mountain. (Poles flock to ski in Austria, not least because the food is familiar.) Anne once spent a few months at the American Academy in Berlin, an amazing institution that operates out of a villa on Lake Wannsee and has its own chef. Once a semester, the chef—who normally worked in the realm of French-Austrian fusion cuisine—would solemnly declare that it was time for "student night" and serve up *Wiener Schnitzel*. This is a dish that is simultaneously scorned and celebrated. It's also a dish that everybody in Central Europe has eaten in his or her youth, and for everybody it brings back memories.

This is not a light or abstemious dish; we would not serve it for a ladies' lunch. However, as the Poles have realized long ago, it makes a terrific Sunday night family dinner, it's not difficult or intimidating, and it can basically be made with things you might be expected to have in your refrigerator or freezer anyway. The addition of onion is not absolutely necessary, strictly speaking, but it's what Poles often do. Serve this dish with mashed potatoes, roasted beets, and pickles; and then play a game of Scrabble to finish off the evening.

4 to 6 boneless pork loin chops
1 cup/110 g store-bought dry or homemade toasted bread crumbs
½ cup/65 g all-purpose flour
Handful of fresh flat-leaf parsley, finely chopped
2 garlic cloves, minced
Salt and freshly ground pepper
2 large eggs, lightly beaten
About ⅓ cup/75 ml light vegetable oil, plus more as needed
1 large onion, peeled, halved, and sliced in half-moons
1 lemon, cut into wedges

Preheat the oven to 200°F/95°C, or turn on a warming oven.

Cut off any visible fat from the pork chops, place them on a cutting board, and pound them flat. You can use a meat pounder or the flat side of a cleaver; a heavy frying pan also works well. (Place the chops between sheets of wax paper if you are worried about shredding or creating holes in the meat.) The cutlets should wind up as thin as possible—about ¼ in/6 mm thick, and almost double their original size. (You can also, of course, ask your butcher to do this.)

Combine the bread crumbs, flour, parsley, and garlic in a shallow bowl and season with salt and pepper. Pour the beaten eggs in a second bowl. Rinse the cutlets and pat dry.

Heat 2 tbsp of the vegetable oil in a large frying pan over medium heat. While the oil gets hot, take the first cutlet, and dip both sides in the beaten eggs. Shake off any excess egg, then dip the cutlet in the bread crumb mix, so that it is entirely coated. Place in the pan and add two or three more breaded cutlets, making sure they fit in the pan without overcrowding. Cook until the outsides are toasted brown and the cutlets are cooked through, about 10 minutes on each side. As they are done, remove them to a shallow baking dish or ovenproof serving dish, and set in the oven to keep warm. Cook the remaining cutlets, adding more oil as needed (you don't want the pan to dry out and have the cutlets stick).

Cook the sliced onion in the frying pan over medium heat, adding a little extra oil if necessary, until translucent. Transfer the cutlets to individual dinner plates or a serving dish, and pour the onion and pan juices on top. Serve with wedges of lemon.

Pork Loin Stuffed with Prunes

SCHAB PIECZONY ZE ŚLIWKAMI

Serves 6 to 8

It's hardly surprising that people who live in a landscape dotted with plum trees should have invented so many different uses for dried plums—otherwise known as prunes. Nor is it surprising that the Poles, who have had a long love affair with pork in all of its forms, would have worked it out that pork needs a touch of sweetness to bring out its best flavor. Several Polish recipes combine pork with fruit, but the most popular combine pork with prunes.

In this recipe, the prunes cook inside the pork, which means that when you slice the loin, each piece comes with an elegant sliver of prune attached. It looks very festive, and isn't at all difficult. The pork loin needs to be boneless, with a pocket or slit cut down the side so that the prunes can go inside the meat. A butcher can do this, but it isn't difficult to do yourself with a sharp knife.

You can, incidentally, make this with *powidła* (plum jam; see the recipe on page 265) instead of prunes. Spread it on rather thickly, but avoid getting too close to the edges so it doesn't leak out. You can also make it with dried apricots and rosemary, instead of prunes and marjoram, though the flavor is then slightly un-Polish.

1 boneless loin of pork (4 to 5 lb/1.8 to 2.3 kg), slit down the side
1 garlic clove, minced
2 tbsp dried marjoram
2 tbsp olive oil
Salt and freshly ground pepper
24 pitted prunes
2 cups/480 ml boiling water

Rinse the pork loin and pat dry.

Combine the garlic, marjoram, olive oil, a large pinch of salt, and several grinds of pepper in a small bowl. Rub the mixture all over the pork loin, including the inside of the pocket, and let sit for 1 hour at room temperature (or you can do this in advance, cover, and refrigerate overnight).

Place the prunes in a mixing bowl and pour the boiling water over them (if the water doesn't cover them, add more). Let sit for 30 minutes, and then drain, reserving the prune-infused water.

When you are ready to start cooking, insert the prunes into the loin pocket, as many as will fit, reserving the rest. Tie up the loin with butcher string in three or four places, just enough so the roast holds together and the prunes stay put.

In a medium Dutch oven just large enough to hold the loin, brown the meat on all sides over medium-high heat. Pour the prune soaking liquid around the meat and scatter any remaining prunes alongside. Cover, bring to a simmer, and continue simmering over low heat until tender and a meat thermometer registers at least 145°F/63°C, about 1½ hours, turning and basting with the pan juices periodically. (If the meat looks too dry, add ½ cup/120 ml of water.)

When the roast is done, remove the meat from the pan and let sit for 10 minutes, tented with foil. Slice thickly and lay out on a platter. Drizzle the slices with a few spoonfuls of the pan juices, and pass the remainder in a sauceboat. Serve immediately.

Roast Pork Tenderloin with Orange and Rosemary

POLĘDWICA WIEPRZOWA W POMARAŃCZACH I ROZMARYNIE

Serves 3 to 4

The Polish love affair with pork has produced an almost infinite array of hams, sausages, and cured meats of every description, which can be grilled, fried, or baked and eaten hot or cold. But a special place in Polish cuisine is nevertheless reserved for pork tenderloin. This, we have found, is the one cut of pork that even people who say they don't like pork often love. It is soft and tender, and not at all dry, as ordinary pork loin sometimes can be. It is very lean and relatively low in fat. Tenderloin is best cooked with a lot of liquid, as well as something sharp and something sweet. Oranges and rosemary—a fabulous combination, which also appears in one of our flavored vodkas (see page 275)—are just the right thing. If you have leftover meat, this is excellent cold the next day, with mustard.

> 1 whole pork tenderloin
> Salt and freshly ground pepper
> 1 cup/240 ml dry white wine, preferably vermouth
> ½ cup/120 ml olive oil
> Zest and juice of ½ orange
> 2 tbsp chopped fresh rosemary
> 2 tbsp orange marmalade, preferably the bitter, chunky kind

Rinse the tenderloin and pat dry. Rub all over with salt and pepper. Curl the meat up at the bottom of a small mixing bowl and pour the wine and olive oil on top, so that the meat is covered (or mostly covered) by the marinade. Let the meat marinate for at least 1 hour at room temperature, turning it over once or twice. (The meat can also be marinated in the refrigerator overnight.)

Preheat the oven to 350°F/180°C/gas 4.

Shake off the marinade and place the meat in a small roasting dish—you can curve it if it is too long to fit—and roast for 40 minutes. The meat should be white on the outside and very pale pink in the center, and a meat thermometer should register 145°F/63°C.

Remove the meat to a carving board and let rest. (Don't worry if it looks pale. This will be rectified by the sauce.) Pour the pan juices into a small saucepan over high heat. Add the orange zest and juice, rosemary, and marmalade. Cook, stirring, until thickened and slightly reduced.

Carve the meat into thin slices and lay them out on a serving platter. Pour the orange-rosemary liquid on top, and serve.

Roast Loin of Wild Boar with Sour Cherries

POLĘDWICA Z DZIKA Z WIŚNIAMI

Serves 8 to 10

To foreigners, there may be no words more intimidating in Polish cooking than "roast wild boar." The phrase conjures up an image of an enormous animal, roasting all day on a spit with an apple in its mouth, perhaps surrounded by picturesque peasants and some noblemen dressed in furs. The good news (or perhaps bad news, if you are a nobleman in furs) is that people haven't cooked a boar that way in Poland for a very long time—unless they were trying to re-create a medieval feast.

Boar meat is part of Polish cuisine for a very good reason: There are a lot of wild boar in Poland. Wild boar are not at all exotic or strange in northern Central Europe, and indeed can be found everywhere from the Grunewald, Berlin's largest park, where they have been known to chase domestic dogs, to Myślęcinek, the park beside the city of Bydogoszcz, near Chobielin. When riding horses in Myślęcinek on the weekends, we sometimes see wallows where they've been rolling in the mud. When we walk through the woods around Chobielin, we sometimes see their delicate hoof prints, too.

In fact, boar meat, like venison, is becoming more and more familiar to North American palates. It's increasingly available in supermarkets, specialty butchers, and farmers' markets in the United States and Western Europe. And no wonder: Think of boar as a superorganic form of free-range pork, and you'll be halfway toward understanding how to cook it. The flavor is smokier and richer than farm-raised pork, but more interesting and certainly leaner. No expert knowledge is required to cook wild boar. The cuts of meat are the same as for pork, and they do not have to be any larger; you can always use half a loin instead of a whole one, for example. Cooking times are thus not necessarily any longer either.

Our recipe, which will surprise you with its effortlessness, provides a spectacular, exotic, and delicious main course for an evening dinner—or a Christmas Day lunch, which is when Anne last served it. The combination of dried sour cherries and smoky meat is sublime. The colors—deep red, earthy brown—are exactly what you want to gaze upon after a morning spent surrounded by wrapping paper and tinsel.

continued

One 750-ml bottle red wine, preferably something robust, like Bordeaux

1 cup/240 ml water

3 whole cloves

3 allspice berries, crushed

5 juniper berries, crushed

10 black peppercorns, crushed

1 celery stalk, trimmed and halved crosswise

1 boneless loin of wild boar (about 2 lb/910 g)

FOR THE SAUCE

2 cups/245 g dried sour cherries (These are usually available in the bulk dried food sections of well-stocked supermarkets.)

1 tbsp sugar

½ cup/120 ml heavy cream

TO MAKE THE MARINADE: In a medium mixing bowl, stir together the wine, water, cloves, allspice berries, juniper berries, peppercorns, and celery.

Place the boar loin in the center of a 9-x-12-in/23-x-30.5-cm roasting pan. Pour the marinade over the loin, cover with a lid or foil, and let sit at room temperature for at least 4 hours, or refrigerate overnight. Turn the meat over in the marinade from time to time.

When ready to cook, preheat the oven to 350°F/180°C/gas 4.

Place the pan with the boar, in its marinade, on the center rack of the oven and cook, covered, for 45 minutes to an hour, depending on the size of your loin; baste or turn it over a couple of times. When done, the meat should be uniformly brown throughout, not pink in the center (a meat thermometer should register at least 145°F/63°C).

Remove the roast from the pan, tent with foil, and let stand on a carving board for 10 to 15 minutes.

TO MAKE THE SAUCE: Strain the marinade into a medium saucepan. Add the sour cherries and sugar and bring to a boil. Turn down the heat and simmer, uncovered, until the marinade has thickened into a sauce. The length of time here will depend on the quantity of juices—you want to reduce the liquid by about one-third, or until it's smooth and silky. Stir in the cream, simmer 1 minute more, and remove from the heat.

Slice the boar loin thinly. Place on a platter, pour the cherry sauce on top, and serve immediately.

CHAPTER FIVE

Pierogi
and
Pancakes

Polish Dumplings
PIEROGI
page 200

Master Pierogi Recipe
page 202

**Potato, Cheese, Bacon,
and Peas Filling**
page 207

**Truffles and Brown
Butter Filling**
page 209

**Wild Mushrooms and
Sauerkraut Filling**
page 210

**Duck and Red Cabbage Filling
with Orange Butter**
page 211

Fruit Pierogi
page 214

**Orange Filling with Ginger
and Cointreau**
page 215

**Strawberry Filling with
Sour Cream and Brown Sugar**
page 217

Apple Latkes
PLACKI Z JABŁKAMI
page 218

Easy Microwave Applesauce
MUS JABŁKOWY Z MIKROFALÒWKI
page 220

Rolled Pancakes with Jam
NALEŚNIKI
page 221

Polish Dumplings

PIEROGI

It is no surprise that the word *pierogi* appears in half a dozen Slavic languages. Wrapping meat, cheese, or fruit inside pasta dough and then dropping the resulting dumpling in a pot of boiling water seems to be one of the oldest ideas in Slavic cooking. And not only Slavic: Pierogi are also made throughout the Baltic states, eastern and southeastern Europe, Germany, and central Asia, though sometimes they go by different names. History has not recorded the nationality of the original inventor, but in the broader scheme of things, they are clearly related to Chinese dumplings—think wontons—and Jewish kreplach and Italian tortellini as well.

In Poland, as in Hungary and Ukraine, pierogi are associated with celebrations: weddings, christenings, first communions, and Christmas. This too is no surprise, since they do take a certain amount of extra effort, some advance preparation, and, if many guests are coming, multiple cooks. Traditionally, groups of women—mothers, daughters, cousins—would stand in the kitchen and talk while chopping onions and making dozens of pierogi the night before the wedding, or the day before a summer party. Thus did the making of the pierogi itself turn into a celebration.

In recent years, the humble pierogi, traditionally stuffed with a bit of minced meat or some farmer's cheese, has grown far more sophisticated. Warsaw restaurants now do delicate, haute cuisine versions, with impossibly thin dough and exotic stuffings. *Pierogarnia*—pierogi bars—have sprung up across the country, offering everything from spinach and mozzarella pierogi to strawberry and banana dessert pierogi.

We include here both a traditional filling—cheese and potato with baby peas, known as "Ruskie," or Russian—as well as a few more exotic versions, for those who want to try something truly different.

To make a dough recipe that was foolproof—and also produced a more delicate casing to complement our exotic fillings—Danielle went to many sources, starting with a Ukrainian friend of mine in Warsaw, and finishing with Paul Grimes, former food editor of *Gourmet*, whom we thank for sharing his Russian grandmother's recipe. The proportions he suggested were excellent: The dough came out perfectly every time and made just the right number of pierogi—16 to 20, or enough for 4 to 6 hungry diners. (To make more, simply double or triple the recipe.)

continued

Master Pierogi Recipe

Serves 4 to 6 (makes 16 to 20 pierogi)

3 cups/390 g all-purpose flour, plus additional for kneading
1 large egg
2 tsp vegetable oil
1 tsp salt, plus more for the boiling water
½ to ¾ cup/120 to 180 ml warm water
Pierogi filling of your choice (see pages 207–217)
3 tbsp unsalted butter, plus more as needed

On a clean work surface, mound the flour and make a well in the center. Add the egg, vegetable oil, and salt to the well and carefully beat together with a fork without incorporating the flour. Continue stirring with a wooden spoon, adding small amounts of the warm water, and gradually incorporating the flour. Only add the next bit of water when the last has been thoroughly blended with the flour and the mixture has become dry. Once the dough has begun to form, lose the spoon and knead the dough with your hands. Stop adding water once all the flour has been incorporated and a soft dough has formed (it should not feel wet or sticky—if it does, add a little more flour). Grab a kitchen timer and set it for 8 minutes. Continue to knead the dough until the timer goes off, dusting the work surface with flour as needed to keep the dough from sticking. It should be smooth and elastic. Invert a bowl over the dough and let it rest at room temperature for 1 hour.

Meanwhile, make the filling and bring a large pot of salted water to a boil.

Roll out the dough on a lightly floured work surface until about ⅛ in/3 mm thick. Cut circles 2 to 3 in/5 to 7.5 cm in diameter with either the rim of a glass or a cookie cutter. Spoon about 1 tbsp of filling in the center of each one, and fold the dough over the filling to make a half circle. (Don't overfill, or the pierogi will become difficult to seal.) Crimp the edges with your fingers or the tines of a fork so they are well sealed (dampen the edges first if necessary).

Boil the pierogi in batches, for 5 minutes *after* they have floated to the surface of the water. Remove from the water with a slotted spoon and set aside on a large plate or platter. In a large frying pan, melt the butter over medium-high heat and lightly brown the cooked pierogi in batches—as many as will fit in the pan without crowding, turning once and adding more butter to the pan if necessary between batches. Transfer to a warm platter, top as directed, and serve immediately.

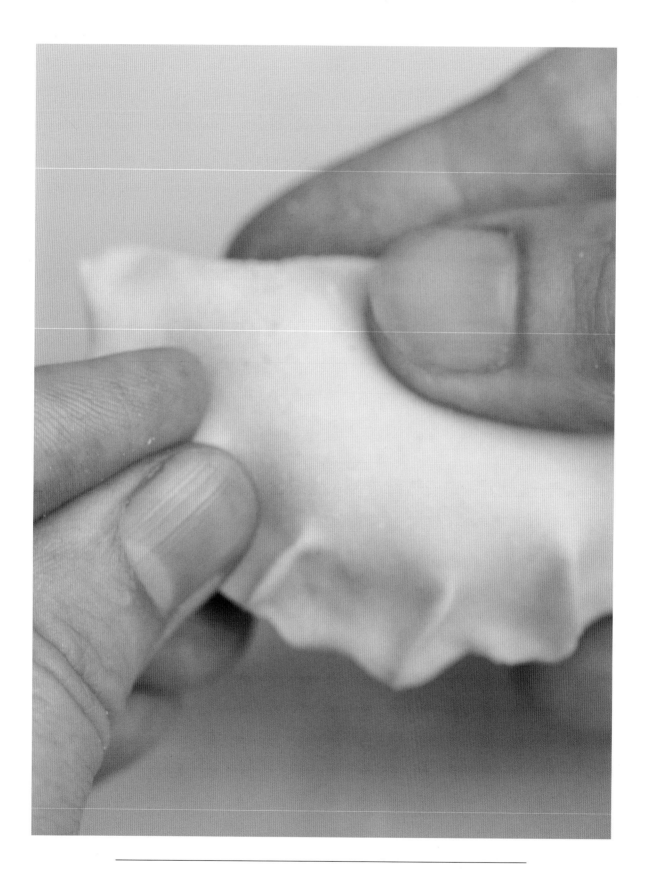

Potato, Cheese, Bacon, and Peas Filling

makes 16 to 20 pierogi

The baby peas are a tasty addition to the standard cheese and potato pierogi familiar to North Americans. If you don't like peas, you can simply omit them. Ditto for the bacon. Because Poles use ricotta in their pierogi, this version is subtly cheesy—but if you like a cheesier taste, add ½ cup/115 g of mild cheddar, Gruyère, or even Parmesan to the filling.

> 2 medium potatoes (white, baking, or Yukon gold—whatever you prefer), peeled and cut into chunks
>
> 6 strips bacon
>
> 3 large onions, peeled—1 minced and 2 sliced
>
> 1 cup/130 g frozen baby peas, defrosted
>
> 9 oz/255 g ricotta cheese
>
> Salt and freshly ground pepper
>
> 2 tbsp unsalted butter, plus more as needed
>
> 1 to 2 cups/240 to 480 ml light sour cream (optional)

Put the potatoes in a large saucepan filled with water, bring to a boil, and continue boiling until soft. Drain and place in a large mixing bowl.

While the potatoes are cooking, fry the bacon in a large frying pan over medium-high heat until crispy. Remove the cooked bacon and drain on paper towels, but keep 1 or 2 tbsp of the fat in the pan. Add the minced onion and cook in the bacon fat until it is soft and lightly browned. Add the peas and continue to cook until the peas are just cooked, about 2 minutes. Set aside.

Crumble the bacon and add it to the bowl with the potatoes, along with the cheese. Season generously with salt and pepper, and mash the ingredients together. We use a hand mixer set at a low speed. You can use a food processor if you wish, but be careful not to overprocess: The mixture should be somewhat lumpy—not creamy smooth. Fold in the peas and minced onions. Taste and correct for seasoning.

Fill and cook the pierogi as directed.

continued

Meanwhile, melt the butter over medium heat in the same frying pan you used for the minced onion. Cook the sliced onions until soft and brown. Do not cook them too quickly; this should take 20 minutes or so. Reduce the heat to low if necessary. When done, set aside and keep them warm. You can cover them with foil and place in a warming oven, or an oven set on low heat.

Pour the cooked onions over the tops of the fried pierogi and serve with a bowl of the sour cream on the side for those who would like to dollop some of that on, too.

Truffles and Brown Butter Filling

makes 16 to 20 pierogi

3 medium Yukon gold potatoes, peeled and cut into chunks
3 tbsp unsalted butter
1 cup/115 g grated Parmigiano-Reggiano
½ cup/120 ml heavy cream
1 whole fresh white or black truffle, or one 1-oz/30-g jarred truffle, shaved into thin slices
Salt and freshly ground pepper

Put the potatoes in a large saucepan, cover with water, and bring to a boil. Continue boiling until soft, drain, and place in a large mixing bowl.

Add 2 tbsp of the butter, the cheese, cream, and half of the truffle slices and season with salt and pepper. Mash together until well mixed.

Fill and cook the pierogi as directed.

Melt the remaining 1 tbsp butter in a small frying pan over medium heat. As the butter begins to brown, quickly stir the rest of the truffle shavings into the butter and pour over the pierogi, tossing to coat before serving.

Wild Mushrooms and Sauerkraut Filling

makes 16 to 20 pierogi

In this recipe, you can skip the step of frying the pierogis. Either way, they're topped with fried onions.

> 2 cups/480 ml boiling water
> One 1-oz/30-g package dried mixed wild mushrooms or porcini
> 6 tbsp/85 g unsalted butter, plus more as needed
> ½ lb/225 g mixed fresh wild mushrooms, cleaned (see Note, page 115), trimmed, and roughly sliced
> 1 lb/455 g sauerkraut, drained
> Salt and freshly ground pepper
> 2 onions, peeled and sliced
> 1 to 2 cups/240 to 480 ml light sour cream

Pour the boiling water over the dried mushrooms in a heat-proof bowl, and set aside for at least 30 minutes. Strain the mushroom liquid through a fine-mesh strainer lined with paper towel or cheesecloth to remove any grit, and set aside 1 cup/240 ml. (Discard the rest or save for another use.) Rinse the rehydrated mushrooms thoroughly and set aside.

Melt 2 tbsp of the butter in a medium Dutch oven over medium-high heat. Cook the fresh mushrooms in the butter until tender, about 10 minutes. Stir in the rehydrated mushrooms, and then the sauerkraut. Raise the heat, pour in the reserved mushroom liquid, and bring to a boil. Lower the heat, cover the pot, and simmer until the sauerkraut is tender, about 20 minutes. If any liquid remains, raise the heat and boil it off. Toss the mixture with 2 tbsp butter and season generously with salt and pepper. Remove to a food processor and pulse the mixture together until finely chopped, but not puréed. There should be a little bit of roughness and texture to the filling.

Fill and cook the pierogi as directed.

Melt the remaining 2 tbsp butter in a large frying pan over medium heat. Fry the sliced onions until soft and golden, about 20 minutes.

Top the pierogi with the onions, and serve the sour cream on the side.

Duck and Red Cabbage Filling with Orange Butter

makes 16 to 20 pierogi

1 duck breast (about ½ lb/225 g; see Note)
1 tbsp dried thyme
½ large head red cabbage
2 tbsp unsalted butter
¼ cup/60 ml dry red wine
½ cup plus 2 tbsp/150 ml chicken stock
⅛ tsp ground cloves
2 tbsp dried cranberries
Salt and freshly ground pepper

FOR THE ORANGE BUTTER
Zest of 1 large navel orange and about half the juice
(¼ cup/60 ml juice)
¼ cup/55 g sugar
½ cup/115 g unsalted butter, diced
3 tbsp Cointreau (orange liqueur)

If using a fresh duck breast, remove the skin and rub the meat all over with the thyme. Set aside. If you wish to fry the pierogi in duck fat instead of butter, you can take the skin, slice it thinly, and fry in a small frying pan over high heat. When the skin is crunchy, like crackling, remove from the rendered fat with a slotted spoon and drain on a paper towel. (You'll use these for a garnish.) Set aside 3 tbsp of the fat.

Core the cabbage and chop roughly. In a large saucepan or Dutch oven, melt 1 tbsp of the butter over medium heat and cook the cabbage until softened, but do not brown (or it will become bitter). Add the wine, chicken stock, and cloves. Bring to a boil, lower the heat, and simmer, uncovered, for 30 minutes, until the cabbage is tender.

Melt the remaining 1 tbsp of butter (you can do this in a small bowl in the microwave). Stir it into the cabbage, add the cranberries, and cook, stirring occasionally, for another 10 minutes.

Chop the duck breast into rough chunks. Combine with the cabbage in a food processor, and add a generous dose of salt and pepper. Pulse the ingredients until they are chopped finely, but be careful not to overprocess them into a paste. Check the seasoning and adjust if necessary.

Fill and cook the pierogi as directed.

continued

TO MAKE THE ORANGE BUTTER: Purée the orange zest and sugar in a food processor. Add the diced butter and purée again until fluffy. Add the orange juice and Cointreau, and process again until creamy. Set aside.

Place a large frying pan over medium-high heat. Swirl in the orange butter, and let bubble for a minute or so until slightly thickened. Return all the pierogi to the pan and toss to coat in the butter.

Spoon the contents of the pan onto a platter, sprinkle with the duck cracklings, if you've made them, and serve. Or, to serve as an elegant appetizer, arrange two or three pierogi on each small plate, and spoon the orange butter over them. Garnish with the cracklings.

NOTE: *If you have any leftover cooked duck from our Duck Breast with Sautéed Pears and Shallots (page 164) or from another recipe, this is an excellent way to use it up. Roughly chop it and put it in the food processor along with the red cabbage.*

Fruit Pierogi

Fresh fruit pierogi are virtually unknown outside of Poland, and yet wrapping seasonal mixtures of fruit in dough makes a delicious dessert. In the summer, when strawberries are bursting with juice, all you need to do is enclose a single strawberry inside each pierogi, boil, and serve with sour cream and brown sugar—or, if you prefer, vanilla ice cream and a drizzle of chocolate syrup.

Traditionally fruit pierogi are eaten boiled, not fried. However, depending on the fruit and your inclinations, you should feel free to try it either way. We have included two suggestions for fruit pierogi—one made with strawberries, and the other with oranges—but you should definitely experiment with other types of fruit. Try blueberry pierogi with lemon curd sauce, or raspberries with vanilla ice cream and framboise (raspberry liqueur) and a sprinkling of chopped mint—whatever appeals to your imagination and taste buds.

Orange Filling with Ginger and Cointreau

makes 16 to 20 pierogi

3 navel oranges
1 small piece fresh ginger (about 2 in/5 cm), peeled and grated
1 tsp sugar
2 tbsp Cointreau (orange liqueur)
½ cup/115 g candied ginger, thinly sliced

With a sharp knife or peeler, peel the oranges down to the fruit, making sure you remove all the white pith. Cut up one of the oranges into small chunks, about ¾ in/2 cm. Toss with a third of the grated ginger and set aside for filling the pierogi.

Slice the remaining two oranges crosswise. Place in a large bowl and toss with the remaining grated ginger, the sugar, and Cointreau. Refrigerate for at least 1 hour, or until ready to serve.

Fill and cook the pierogi as directed. Let cool.

Toss the pierogi with the sliced oranges and Cointreau and spoon onto a large platter. Sprinkle with the candied ginger slices and serve.

SERVING VARIATION: *Put a scoop of the finest dark chocolate ice cream you can find in each dessert bowl. Divide the pierogi and orange slices among the bowls, and spoon some of the Cointreau-flavored juice on each one. Sprinkle with the candied ginger and serve.*

Strawberry Filling with Sour Cream and Brown Sugar

makes 16 to 20 pierogi

2 pints/715 g fresh strawberries, hulled
2 tbsp vodka
1 tbsp granulated sugar
Sour cream for serving
Brown sugar for serving

Sort out how many strawberries you will need for the number of pierogi you are making: You want 1 strawberry for each pierogi, or if large, ½ strawberry. Set aside.

Halve the remaining strawberries, or quarter if large, and toss with the vodka and granulated sugar in a large mixing bowl. Cover and marinate in the refrigerator (you can do this several hours in advance, if you prefer).

Fill and cook the pierogi as directed.

Distribute the pierogi evenly among dessert plates or bowls. Toss the marinating strawberries once more, and top the warm pierogi with a serving of strawberries and their syrup. Dollop on sour cream and a good sprinkling of brown sugar and serve.

SERVING VARIATION: *Omit the sour cream and brown sugar and instead arrange the pierogi and strawberries atop very fine dark chocolate or vanilla ice cream, and add chocolate syrup if you like.*

Apple Latkes

PLACKI Z JABŁKAMI

Serves 4 to 6

These apple pancakes aren't really pancakes, in the American sense of the word, but something closer to apple fritters—or, to be even more precise, apple latkes. The apples are not made into a filling and then tucked into the cooked pancakes, but rather are grated directly into the batter. This is an ideal dish for a special breakfast, if you've got guests or just want something festive in the morning. But in Anne's house apple pancakes are also served for children's supper, or even adult supper, on evenings when something fast and delicious is required.

This is Anne's mother-in-law's recipe, and she would not even dare to make it if her mother-in-law, whose expertise in this area cannot be challenged, were around. A recipe for homemade applesauce, to be eaten alongside the pancakes, follows. Leftover pancakes can be stored in the refrigerator for a day or so, and reheated before eating. Anne's children also eat them cold right out of a lunchbox.

> 2 apples, peeled and coarsely grated
> 1 cup/130 g all-purpose flour
> ½ cup/120 ml plain low-fat yogurt or kefir
> 2 large eggs, lightly beaten
> ½ cup/120 ml water
> Pinch of salt
> 1 to 2 tbsp grapeseed or vegetable oil, plus more as needed
> Confectioners' sugar for sprinkling
> Easy Microwave Applesauce (page 220) for serving

Put the apples, flour, and yogurt in a mixing bowl and mix with a wooden spoon. Add the eggs and stir. Add the water and salt and mix again.

Heat a large frying pan over medium heat, and spread just enough of the oil over the bottom to cover it thinly. (If you use too much oil, the pancakes can become rather greasy.) Drop a heaping 1 tbsp of the batter onto the pan for each pancake, and don't let them touch one another. They should be thick and chunky, like blini or latkes. Cook on one side until the bottom is golden, 3 to 5 minutes, depending on how hot your pan is, and then flip.

As the pancakes are cooked, place them on a plate covered with a paper towel to absorb any grease. If you are making large numbers of them, place them in layers, with paper towel in between. (Remove the paper towels before serving.)

Place the pancakes on a platter or individual plates and sprinkle with confectioners' sugar. Accompany each serving with a heaping spoonful of applesauce.

continued

FROM A POLISH COUNTRY HOUSE KITCHEN

218

Easy Microwave Applesauce
MUS JABŁKOWY Z MIKROFALÒWKI

Serves 4 to 6

We don't know why people buy applesauce when it is so easy to make. This recipe can be halved or doubled very easily, depending on how much of it you need. Use whatever type of apple you prefer—if you like a more tart sauce, you can use a Granny Smith, for example.

3 apples, cored, peeled, and coarsely chopped
1 tbsp sugar
1 tsp ground cinnamon

Place the diced apples in a microwave-safe bowl, and pour in just enough water to cover. Microwave at high power for 3 to 5 minutes, depending on the strength of your oven. The apples should come out soft, and most of the water should have boiled off. If this is not the case, return them for another minute.

Mash the apples with a fork, and mix in the sugar and cinnamon. Serve immediately.

Rolled Pancakes with Jam

NALEŚNIKI

Serves 6 to 7 (makes about 15 pancakes)

We know that we've just said that apple pancakes (see page 218) aren't really much like American pancakes. And the truth is that these *naleśniki* aren't either. The word *naleśniki* does translate as "pancakes," but these are closer to French crêpes, and closer still to Hungarian *palacsinta*: They are thinner and more limp than American pancakes, and are meant to be folded around something, not eaten in a stack with maple syrup.

There are savory versions—you can wrap them around a chicken sauce, or some grilled vegetables. But we think the pancakes work best with Polish Plum Jam (*Powidła*), which is thick, sticky, and not too sweet. Eaten with jam (or with butter and sugar), they make an excellent breakfast, or even a light supper. Inevitably they are the thing you make when there's nothing in the house except eggs and flour, which happens to everybody from time to time.

> 1 cup/240 ml plain low-fat yogurt
> 2 large eggs
> ½ cup/120 ml cold water
> 1 cup/130 g all-purpose flour
> Pinch of salt
> 1 to 2 tbsp grapeseed or vegetable oil, plus more as needed
> Plum Jam (*Powidła*, page 265) or another jam
> (or butter and sugar or applesauce) for serving

Place the yogurt, eggs, water, flour, and salt in a large mixing bowl and whisk until the batter is very smooth. You can also do this in a blender or food processor if you'd prefer, but it should not be necessary. The batter should be well blended and the consistency of light cream.

Cover the batter with plastic wrap and refrigerate. (This allows the flour to absorb some of the liquid, and it makes the batter lighter.) If you've got time, leave the batter in the refrigerator for 1 or 2 hours. If not, 20 minutes should do it.

continued

Heat a small frying pan or a crêpe pan, if you've got one, over low heat and spread just enough of the oil over the bottom to cover it thinly. (You can also do this with a brush.) When the pan is heated, pour in enough of the batter—about ¼ cup/60 ml for a standard crêpe pan—so that it makes a thin, smooth film covering the entire pan. Cook over low heat, occasionally shaking the pan. Lift up the edges to check the pancake; when it is lightly browned, usually about 2 minutes, flip it over, either by gripping an edge with your fingers, or with a spatula. (Or, of course, flip it in the air like they do in the movies, if you dare.) Cook for 2 minutes more, or until lightly browned. The finished pancake should be thin, but not at all fragile.

Treat the first pancake as an experiment; if it has cooked too fast, lower the heat. If the batter seems too thick, beat in 1 tsp water, and add another if necessary. As they are done, stack the pancakes on a plate covered with a paper towel to absorb any oil. Keep them warm if you can, but these are usually eaten at room temperature, so they needn't be very hot.

These are always served with something rolled up inside them. *Powidła* is the traditional thing, but you can use another type of jam, butter and sugar, applesauce, or anything, really. Let children put the spreads on themselves. You are allowed to pick them up and eat them with your fingers.

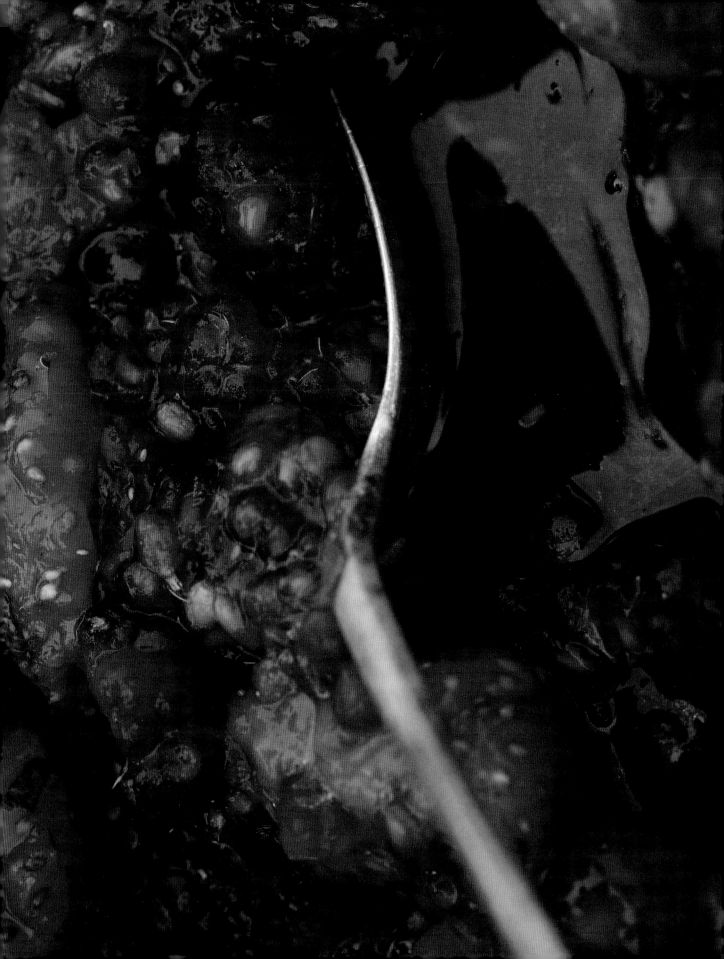

CHAPTER SIX

Desserts

Gingerbread Cookies
PIERNICZKI
page 228

Gingerbread Cake
PIERNIK
page 231

Plum Cake
PLACEK
page 233

Orange-Saffron Rum Cake
BABKA RUMOWA
page 234

Lithuanian Honey Cake
MIÓDOWNIK STAROLITEWSKI
page 236

**Cheesecake with Strawberry–
Red Currant Sauce**
SERNIK Z POLEWĄ Z TRUSKAWEK
I CZERWONYCH PORZECZEK
page 239

Poppy-Seed Torte
TORT MAKOWY
page 242

Two Mazureks
DWA MAZURKI
page 245

Orange and Almond Mazurek
MAZUREK POMARAŃCZOWY
page 247

Chocolate Mazurek
MAZUREK CZEKOLADOWY
page 248

**Mini-Meringues with
Fresh Berries and Crème Fraîche**
MINIPAVLOVA ZE ŚWIEŻYMI
OWOCAMI
page 250

Spicy Oranges
PIKANTNE POMARANCZE
page 252

Red Fruit Salad
CZERWONA SAŁATKA
OWOCOWA
page 255

Gingerbread Cookies

PIERNICZKI

Makes about 3 dozen cookies, depending on the size

The point of these cookies is to make them in large quantities, a few days before Christmas, and then to eat them all the way through to the New Year. They are meant to be on the hard and crunchy side, which is why they last. They can then be served with spicy ginger tea on a cold afternoon, when unexpected guests come to visit.

These are also, incidentally, the cookies Anne makes to hang on her tree. To make them for yours, punch a hole in the cookies before baking—the top of a ball-point pen works perfectly—then bake, decorate excessively, add a hook or thread, and hang.

1¼ cups/280 g unsalted butter

½ cups/120 ml honey

1 cup/225 g packed brown sugar

1 tsp vegetable oil

2 tbsp unsweetened cocoa powder

2 tbsp ground cinnamon

2 tbsp ground cloves

2 tbsp nutmeg, freshly grated if possible

2 tbsp ground ginger

Pinch of salt

Pinch of freshly ground pepper

2 tbsp peeled and minced fresh ginger

2½ tbsp vanilla sugar, or 1 tbsp vanilla extract

4½ cups/585 g all-purpose flour

½ tsp baking soda

2½ tsp baking powder

6 large eggs, at room temperature

Dried fruits for decorating (raisins, chopped dried apricots, candied orange peel)

Sliced almonds for decorating

Confectioners' sugar for dusting

continued

In the microwave, melt the butter with the honey in a microwave-safe bowl. Pour into a large mixing bowl, add the brown sugar and vegetable oil, and stir. Add the cocoa powder, spices, salt and pepper, fresh ginger, and vanilla sugar. Mix well and let cool for a few minutes.

Whisk together the flour, baking soda, and baking powder in a large bowl and add to the brown sugar and honey mixture. Stir in the eggs. Mix well, first with a wooden spoon, then by hand. Mold the dough into a ball, cover with plastic wrap, and leave at room temperature for 24 hours (or up to 48 hours, if you don't want to make right away).

When ready to bake, preheat the oven to 300°F/150°C/gas 2.

Roll out the dough as thin as it will go without breaking (this recipe doesn't require a floured surface), and cut into shapes. If you haven't got cookie cutters, then use an upside-down wine glass to make circles or half-moons.

Now decorate! The traditional thing is to use dried fruits and nuts, but you can also use store-bought sprinkles, which Anne's children prefer. Dust with confectioners' sugar, if so desired, as well. (There is no such thing as a tacky gingerbread cookie.) To make the decorations stay on better, roll over each cookie once with a rolling pin before placing on an ungreased cookie sheet.

If these are really thin, they should bake only 7 to 8 minutes, but if you haven't quite managed that, leave them in for 10 minutes. They should turn a darker color on top. Cool the cookies on a wire rack. Store in an airtight container for up to 10 days.

Gingerbread Cake

PIERNIK

Serves 6 to 8

The city of Toruń is about an hour's drive from Chobielin, and Anne often takes her guests there for lunch. They go for the architecture—Toruń was never damaged during World War II, like so many Polish cities, and still has lovely medieval churches and baroque houses—and to see the home of Copernicus, the city's most famous resident. But they also go for the *pierniczki*, the gingerbread cookies, which are Toruń's most famous culinary specialty. There is even a gingerbread museum in town, where they show you how gingerbread was traditionally made and explain its history.

Toruń was an important medieval port and trading city, and in the Middle Ages (and indeed later on) the city was a hub for the importation of spices. Back then, cinnamon, ginger, nutmeg, and cloves, which came from the Far East, were exotic curiosities, and gingerbread was a fantastically expensive luxury good. Gingerbread cookies and cakes were made into elaborate forms and shapes, which were often given as presents on special occasions. Though cinnamon is no longer worth its weight in gold, a little bit of that tradition remains, and *torunskie pierniki*, Toruń gingerbread, still comes in an amazing array of forms and shapes.

What follows is a recipe for *piernik*, gingerbread cake, which is a little more luscious than the cookies in the previous recipe. The cake goes wonderfully with coffee, and is perfect for serving in the afternoon as well as after dinner.

continued

1 cup/225 g unsalted butter, softened, plus some extra to grease the pan

2 cups/200 g confectioners' sugar

8 large eggs, at room temperature, separated

2¼ cups/540 ml honey

1 tsp ground ginger

Pinch of ground cloves

Pinch of ground nutmeg

3¼ cups/445 g pastry flour

1 tsp baking powder

2 tbsp finely chopped walnuts

2 tbsp finely chopped almonds

2 tbsp finely chopped candied orange peel

FOR THE FROSTING

1 cup/225 g unsalted butter

2 tbsp cold water

1 cup/225 g granulated sugar

¼ cup/20 g cocoa powder

2 tbsp Cognac or another brandy

TO MAKE THE CAKE: Preheat the oven to 350°F/180°C/gas 4. Butter a 9-in/23-cm pan. (This can be a babka—or Bundt—pan, a tube pan, a springform cake pan, or an ordinary square pan).

Put the softened butter in a large mixing bowl and add the confectioners' sugar. Using a wooden spoon, mix together, and then add the egg yolks, one by one. Make sure everything is thoroughly mixed. Add the honey, spices, and pastry flour and mix some more. Finally add the baking powder, nuts, and orange peel and stir. The mixture isn't supposed to be smooth, but it should be well blended.

In a separate bowl, beat the egg whites with an electric mixer at medium speed until they hold soft peaks. Carefully fold the egg whites into the batter. Pour the batter into the pan, filling it about halfway.

Bake for 40 minutes to 1 hour, or until a toothpick inserted into the center comes out clean. Cool the cake in the pan on a rack. When the cake is cool, remove from the pan if you've made it in a round pan. If you've made the cake in a square pan, cut it into serving pieces and place them on a rack.

TO MAKE THE FROSTING: Place the butter in a saucepan over medium heat, pour in the cold water, and add the sugar and cocoa power. Stir, raise the heat to high, and bring to a boil. Lower heat and keep at a low boil for 5 minutes. Remove from the heat and, mixing steadily, pour in the Cognac.

Pour the frosting immediately over the cake or over individual pieces. The frosting should drip down the sides in rivulets. Serve immediately.

Plum Cake

PLACEK

Serves 6 to 8

This is, we suspect, one of those recipes whose origins lie, once again, in the long relationship between Poland and France. Anne is pretty sure she had something exactly like it as a teenager, when she spent a month living with a family in France, and she's also pretty sure that what she had then was clafoutis.

This is, in essence, plums baked into a kind of cake or pudding. Here, as in all recipes made with plums, Poles would use damsons, the elongated cooking plums (discussed at greater length in the recipe for Plum Jam, *Powidła*, page 265). But this recipe will work with other kinds of plums, too, including the sweet juicy ones, as well as with cherries, pear slices, and even blackberries.

Poles would eat this unadorned. But we like to do as the English do, and pour a little heavy cream on top. A dollop of whipped cream goes nicely as well.

½ cup/115 g unsalted butter, softened
1 cup/225 g sugar, plus 1 tbsp
1 cup/130 g all-purpose flour
1 tsp baking powder
Pinch of salt
2 large eggs, at room temperature
About 6 medium plums, skin left on, halved and pitted
Juice of ½ lemon
Ground cinnamon for sprinkling

Preheat the oven to 325°F/165°C/gas 3. Lightly oil a 9-in/23-cm nonstick spring-form pan.

In a medium mixing bowl, cream the butter and 1 cup/225 g sugar together with an electric mixer at medium speed. Beat in the flour, baking powder, and salt. Add the eggs, and beat well until the batter is creamy and smooth.

Spoon the batter into the prepared pan. Place the plums cut-side down in the batter.

Sprinkle the batter with the 1 tbsp sugar, lemon juice, and enough cinnamon to lightly color the top.

Bake for about 1 hour. Cool in the pan, remove the sides, and serve.

Orange-Saffron Rum Cake

BABKA RUMOWA

Serves 10 to 12

Allegedly, babkas got their name from their shape, which resembles that of an old lady's long skirts. *Babka* means "grandmother" in Polish, and indeed, there is something old-fashioned and feminine about these cakes, which are sometimes known as Bundt cakes, from the German, *bundkuchen*. Anne's grandmother used to make babkas, which she would then pack into boxes and send to Anne's family in the mail. She lived in Bessemer, Alabama, and was born in the United States, but her parents were—she thought—from Vilnius. At the time they left, in the second half of the nineteenth century, Vilnius was part of the Russian empire, so she always described them as coming from Russia. In fact Vilnius, now the capital of Lithuania, was at that time a Polish-Jewish city, where business was transacted in Polish and Yiddish. And so in some indirect way, her cakes were probably of Polish origin, too.

Re-creating the grandmother's babka recipe was not easy, however, as she died some years ago. We had several recipes from friends and from Polish cookbooks, but they never seemed to come out right. Whatever worked in Poland didn't seem to taste the same in Washington. It was only when our friend Meghan Gurdon, a champion baker, really put her mind to it that we figured this one out. By our count, she made seven rum babkas before finding the one whose taste passed the ultimate test: Her five children happily ate it up.

You do need a babka or Bundt pan here. Because all of the ingredients must be room temperature, it's important to remember to take the eggs, milk, and butter out of the refrigerator well in advance of making the cake. You can serve it with a simple dusting of confectioners' sugar, but it's delicious if you cover it with the orange glaze. The hint of saffron in this recipe gives the cake a whiff of exoticism, distinguishing it from more ordinary babkas.

2¼ cups/290 g all-purpose flour

¾ cup/170 g sugar

Pinch of salt

1 tbsp yeast granules

1 cup/240 ml milk, at room temperature or warmed slightly

1 cup/225 g raisins, rinsed with water

2 tbsp rum

Pinch of saffron

Zest and juice of 1 medium orange

½ cup/115 g unsalted butter, softened

5 egg yolks, at room temperature

½ cup/120 ml sour cream, at room temperature

1 tsp vanilla extract

About 1 tbsp fine dry bread crumbs for coating the Bundt pan

FOR THE GLAZE (OPTIONAL)

½ cup/110 g sugar

½ cup/120 ml orange juice

Grated orange zest (optional)

Confectioners' sugar for dusting

TO MAKE THE CAKE: Combine 1 tsp of the flour, 1 tsp of the sugar, and the salt in a small bowl. Add the yeast and milk and mix thoroughly. Allow to rest, uncovered, in a warm place.

Combine the raisins, rum, and saffron in a small bowl. Sprinkle with the orange zest and set aside.

Using an electric mixer set at medium speed, cream the butter and remaining sugar in a large bowl until pale and fluffy. Mix in the egg yolks, one at a time, and then stir in the sour cream and vanilla until well combined. Add the remaining flour and the yeast mixture and mix well. Stir in the rum and raisins. Place a kitchen towel over the bowl, and put it in a warm place to rest for 30 minutes.

In the meantime, preheat the oven to 350°F/180°C/gas 4. Grease a Bundt or babka pan with butter and sprinkle with the bread crumbs. Pour the cake batter into the pan, which should be about two-thirds full. Again let sit for about 30 minutes, covered with a kitchen towel.

Place the cake in the oven and bake it for 30 minutes, or until a toothpick inserted in the center comes out clean. Cool for several minutes in the pan, and turn upside down onto a serving plate.

IF MAKING THE GLAZE: Bring all ingredients to a boil in a small saucepan over high heat. Boil until the sugar dissolves—2 to 3 minutes.

Pour the glaze over the warm cake. When the cake is cool, whether it's glazed or not, sift confectioners' sugar all over the top before serving.

Lithuanian Honey Cake

MIÓDOWNIK STAROLITEWSKI

Serves 10 to 12

Things that are called "Lithuanian" in Polish cooking often involve honey (note the recipe for Spicy Lithuanian Vodka on page 276). The Lithuanians were famous beekeepers, and before the Polish king Jagiełło helped convert them to Christianity in 1387, the Lithuanians had a bee goddess. Poland was once the imperial power in Lithuania, and in the eastern part of the country, it's hard to say where Polish customs end and Lithuanian customs begin. Elaborately carved beehives, for example, are a feature of both the Polish and Lithuanian landscape.

Nowadays Poles treat honey like an herb, and reckon it has medicinal properties. So it's not surprising that they like to keep bees in their gardens. Ride a bike for a few miles down the road from Chobielin, and you'll see many gardens with beehives. Anne did build one several years ago, but the bee colony didn't thrive. She was told that it had to do with prevailing winds, the microclimate that makes her garden slightly cooler than the surrounding area, or the proximity of the river. Who knows.

In Jewish homes, honey cake is eaten on the New Year and at Passover, when it is made with matzoh meal and potato flour instead of wheat flour. This version uses wheat flour, and it comes out slightly damp and heavy. It is just what you want after a winter dinner of soup and salad.

> 1¼ cups/300 ml honey
>
> 1 tsp baking soda
>
> 2¼ cups/290 g all-purpose flour
>
> 3 large eggs, separated, at room temperature
>
> 1 cup/225 g sugar
>
> 1 cup/240 ml sour cream
>
> ½ tsp ground cloves
>
> ½ tsp ground cinnamon
>
> ½ tsp ground nutmeg
>
> ½ tsp ground ginger

Preheat the oven to 350°F/180°C/gas 4. Grease the sides of a 9-in/23-cm spring-form pan (or use a nonstick pan), and line the bottom with parchment paper.

In a small saucepan, bring the honey to a boil and let cool. Meanwhile, in a medium bowl, whisk the baking soda with the flour. In a large mixing bowl, beat the egg yolks with the sugar, using a wooden spoon or an electric mixer at medium speed, until the sugar dissolves. Add the sour cream and keep mixing. Slowly incorporate the honey, spices, and the flour and baking soda, mixing all the while.

In another medium bowl, beat the egg whites with an electric mixer at medium speed until they are very stiff. Carefully fold into the batter. Pour the batter into the prepared pan and bake for 45 minutes to 1 hour, until a toothpick inserted in the center comes out cleanish. The cake is meant to be damp, but not actually liquid, in the center. Cool completely in the pan, set on a rack. Remove from the pan and serve.

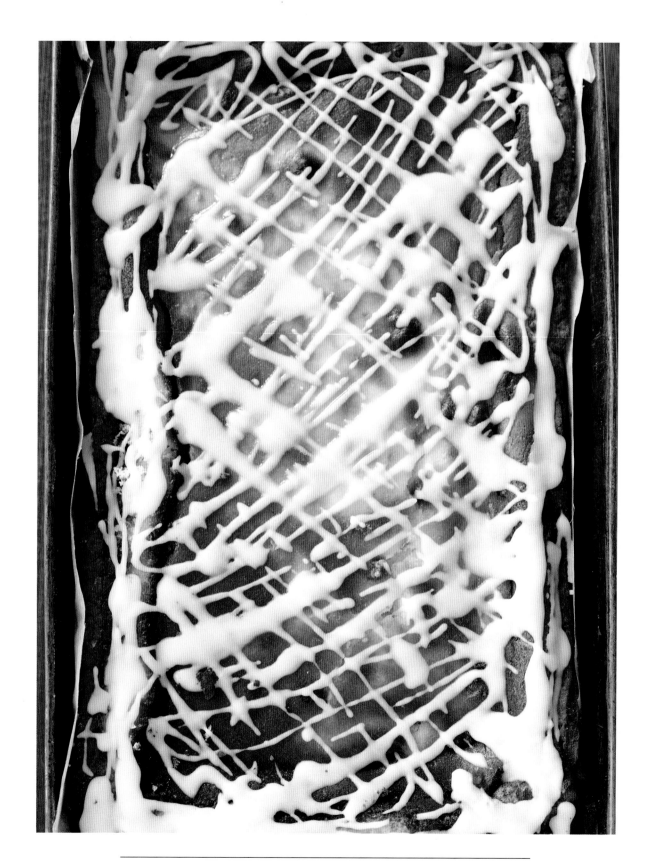

Cheesecake with Strawberry–Red Currant Sauce

SERNIK Z POLEWĄ Z TRUSKAWEK I CZERWONYCH PORZECZEK

Serves 10 to 12

While there is something compelling about the supersweet concoction that Americans call "cheesecake," don't imagine that is the only version around. A Polish cheesecake, or *sernik*, isn't necessarily very sweet or very heavy. Part of the difference is in the cheese: The classic New York version is made with cream cheese, but the Polish version is made with what is sometimes called "pot cheese," and sometimes "farmer's cheese." If you can get this very light, simple cheese, so much the better. If not, we found that ricotta makes an excellent substitute.

We tried various recipes for cheesecake (including a very good but intimidating one sent to Anne by the owners of the tiny, fabulous pastry shop, Femme Fatale, on the ground floor of her building on Grzybowska Street in Warsaw). This particular recipe was inspired by Romka Kachelska, a wonderful cook who for many years kept house for the parish priest of Inowrocław, who happened to be Anne's husband's uncle. Because they never know who might turn up and who might need to be given tea, priests have to have cakes and sweets on hand at all times. And thus Romka's job involved, among other things, making a cheesecake every other week or so. We've changed it somewhat, under the influence of James Beard and others, to suit non-Polish palates.

This is a very light, simple cake, which goes well with ice cream. We like to serve it with a strawberry–red currant sauce, which adds an acidic punch. You can also serve it simply with whipped cream or a light sour cream glaze (see the variation). Don't be put off by the raisins; they're chopped up so they lend their taste without their texture, for those who are not fond of raisins in cakes.

FOR THE BREAD CRUMB CRUST

1½ cups/160 g fine dry bread crumbs

¼ cup/20 g confectioners' sugar, sifted

6 tbsp/85 g unsalted butter, melted

FOR THE FILLING

¾ cup/130 g raisins

1 tbsp all-purpose flour

1½ lb/680 g whole-milk ricotta cheese, at room temperature

4 large eggs, at room temperature

1 cup/225 g granulated sugar

1½ tsp vanilla extract

continued

½ cup/120 ml water

1 cup/225 g fresh strawberries, hulled

¾ cup/170 g fresh red currants or thawed frozen red currants

Preheat the oven to 300°F/150°C/gas 2. Line the bottom of a 9-in/23-cm springform pan with parchment paper (even if using a nonstick pan) and butter the sides.

TO MAKE THE CRUST: Combine the bread crumbs and confectioners' sugar in a medium bowl, and drizzle the melted butter on top. Stir until well mixed. Press the mixture lightly with your fingers into the base of the pan and up the sides a bit, using wax paper or parchment paper, if you like, as a barrier between fingers and crust. Bake for 15 minutes—it will have a somewhat dry, firm appearance when ready—and cool completely before filling.

TO MAKE THE FILLING: Put the raisins in a food processor, sprinkle with the flour, and process until the raisins are nicely chopped. Put the ricotta in a medium bowl, stir in the raisins, and set aside.

With an electric mixer at medium speed, beat the eggs in a large mixing bowl until they are pale yellow. Then, while still beating, slowly add the granulated sugar and vanilla. Stir in the ricotta mixture by hand and continue stirring until the filling is well combined.

Pour the filling into the baked crust and bake for 40 to 50 minutes, until a toothpick inserted in the center comes out clean. Cool completely in the pan. Remove the sides of the pan and transfer the cake to a serving platter.

TO MAKE THE SAUCE: Combine the water and fruit in a microwave-safe dish, and microwave on high for at least 5 minutes. The water should be boiling, but should not evaporate completely. (Alternatively, bring them to a boil in a saucepan, and boil for at least 1 minute).

Remove from the microwave and blend with an immersion blender or in a food processor until thick and smooth, though there will still be visible seeds. Pour the mixture through a fine-mesh strainer into a bowl, straining out the seeds and pushing the fruit through with a wooden spoon until all the juices have been extracted. That's it—the mixture in the bowl is the sauce. Cut the cake into individual pieces and drizzle the sauce over the top, or serve on the side.

VARIATION: *Make the cheesecake, omitting the strawberry–red currant sauce. Combine 2 tbsp sour cream and ¾ cup/60 g confectioners' sugar in a small saucepan over medium-low heat and stir until warm and smooth. Remove from the heat and stir in ¼ tsp milk and a dash of vanilla extract. Drizzle extravagantly all over the cheesecake before serving.*

Poppy-Seed Torte

TORT MAKOWY

Serves 10 to 12

Poppy-seed cakes are ubiquitous in Poland, and are a traditional part of both Polish and Jewish (and indeed Central European) cooking. The most famous Polish poppy-seed cake is the *makowiec*, which is eaten with special gusto at Christmas. The most famous Jewish poppy-seed cake is probably the traditional *hamantaschen*, the triangular pastry that is eaten at Purim. Since the former is tricky to cook at home, and the latter often come out hard and dry, we've decided, instead, to include a recipe for poppy-seed torte, which is perfectly straightforward and equally delicious.

This recipe calls for soaking the poppy seeds in advance. While it is tempting to skip this stage—and possibly hard to find a strainer fine enough for them—it's worth doing if you can, because it makes the seeds softer, so they provide less of a contrast with the cake. (The easiest way to strain the poppy seeds is to use a regular strainer lined with cheesecloth.) We've also noted that in Poland, poppy seeds are ground in a food processor or with a meat grinder before they are used. But poppy seeds are often sold preground now, and they would be worth seeking out.

¾ cup/170 g poppy seeds

6 large eggs, separated, plus 6 egg yolks, at room temperature

1 cup/225 g sugar

½ tsp ground cinnamon

½ tsp ground cloves

½ tsp ground nutmeg

½ tsp grated orange zest

½ cup/115 g blanched and peeled almonds, finely ground in a food processor

¼ cup/20 g confectioners' sugar

continued

Preheat the oven to 350°F/180°C/gas 4. Line the bottom of a 9-in/23-cm spring-form pan with parchment paper, even if it's nonstick, and butter the sides.

Place the poppy seeds in a heat-proof medium mixing bowl, and cover with boiling water. Lit sit for 5 minutes, and drain in a fine-mesh strainer lined with cheesecloth until dry. (If your poppy seeds aren't preground, place them in a food processor or spice grinder and whizz until they are smooth—but not powdery.)

In a medium mixing bowl, beat the egg whites with an electric mixer on medium speed until they are very stiff, and set aside.

In the top of a double boiler, with water simmering in the bottom over low heat, whisk the egg yolks with the sugar until thick and pale yellow. Add the poppy seeds, spices, and orange zest and whisk to combine. Remove from the heat and fold in the egg whites and almonds.

Pour the batter into the prepared pan and bake for 45 minutes to 1 hour, until a toothpick inserted in the center comes out clean. Cool the cake in the pan, set on a rack. Remove the cake from the pan and sprinkle the confectioners' sugar on top before serving.

Two Mazureks

DWA MAZURKI

A *mazurek* is an Easter cake, and part of the point of it is the decoration. It's a very simple cake—more like a big cookie with icing or dried fruit and nuts on top—and it's presented at the end of the Easter breakfast (after the *żurek*, or bread soup, and a vast spread of hams, cheeses, and sausages) with a great flourish.

Allegedly, the *mazurek*, like Spicy Oranges (page 252), comes from Turkey. Supposedly, the decorations are meant to remind you of a Turkish carpet. More to the point, the *mazurek* is also the name of a Polish dance, better known in English as the "mazurka." Chopin wrote several of them.

While you are welcome to make your *mazurek* elegant and sophisticated (and we think our recipes fit that bill), it's also okay to draw a dove with an olive branch in its beak on top of the cake, or to spell out the word "Alleluia" with store-bought icing and raisins. A *mazurek* requires no special skills in baking. Polish children make and decorate *mazurki* with their mothers (much the way American children make brownies) in preparation for Easter.

continued

Orange and Almond Mazurek
MAZUREK POMARAŃCZOWY

Serves 6 to 8

2 cups/290 g blanched and peeled almonds,
finely ground in a food processor
3 cups/675 g sugar
Juice of 1 lemon, plus 1 lemon
2 navel oranges
½ cup/120 ml water
Sliced almonds, for garnish (optional)

Preheat the oven to 225°F/110°C/gas ¼. In a medium mixing bowl, blend 1 cup/ 225 g of the almonds, the sugar, and the lemon juice together. The result should be a dry but spreadable paste. Grease the sides of a 9-in/23-cm round springform pan (or use a nonstick pan), and line the bottom with parchment paper, so the paper comes about 1½ in/4 cm up the sides. Spread the almond mixture evenly over the bottom of the pan, and bake for 15 to 20 minutes. It should be firm but not brown. Cool in the pan. Unlock the sides of the pan and slide the shell onto a serving plate.

Cut the oranges and lemon into quarters, and remove any pits from the lemon. Using the grater attachment on a food processor, grate the fruit together, including the peel.

Combine the water and remaining 2 cups/450 g sugar in a small saucepan, bring to a simmer, and cook, stirring, until the syrup is thick, about 10 minutes.

Pour the fruit and syrup into a large bowl, and using a wooden spoon, mix the ingredients until they start to turn white.

Spread the filling over the baked shell, refrigerate until cold. Garnish with sliced almonds, if desired, and serve.

Chocolate Mazurek
MAZUREK CZEKOLADOWY
Serves 6 to 8

1½ cups/220 g blanched and peeled almonds

½ cup/115 g unsalted butter, softened

1 cup/230 g sugar

4 large eggs, lightly beaten

3 cups/390 g all-purpose flour, plus 1½ tsp

¼ lb/115 g good-quality bittersweet chocolate, grated,
plus extra for decoration

Preheat the oven to 350°F/180°C/gas 4. Grease the sides of a 9-in/23-cm round tart pan (or use a nonstick pan), preferably with a removable bottom. Line the bottom with parchment paper.

Toast the almonds in a small skillet over medium heat. Be careful not to let them burn. When cool, chop them in a food processor until they are finely ground.

In a large mixing bowl, cream the butter with an electric mixer on medium speed. Add 1 cup/145 g of the almonds, and set aside the rest for the topping. Beat in ½ cup/115 g of the sugar and 2 of the eggs, and on low speed, beat in the 3 cups/390 g of the flour. Continue mixing until a dough is formed.

On a floured work surface, roll out the dough until it is about ¼ in/6 mm thick, and large enough to cover the bottom and come slightly up the sides of the prepared pan. Lift the rolled-out dough as best you can and transfer to the pan, pressing the dough with your fingers into bottom and up the sides. Use leftover bits of dough to plug any holes with your fingers. Use foil or parchment to line the shell, then add pastry weights or, as we sometimes do, an ovenproof, flat lid of a small saucepan to weigh down the center of the dough.

Bake the shell for 10 minutes. Remove the weights and bake for another 5 minutes, or until the center no longer feels soft. Remove from the oven and cool in the pan.

Lower the oven temperature to 225°F/110°C/gas ¼.

In a large mixing bowl, using an electric mixer, beat the remaining eggs and ½ cup/115 g sugar together on medium speed until thoroughly blended. Add the chocolate and continue beating for a few more minutes until creamy. Add the 1½ tsp flour, mix thoroughly, and then add the reserved ground almonds, beating until all the ingredients are combined.

Spread the filling over the baked shell and bake for 30 minutes, or until set. Let cool. Remove the tart from the pan and transfer to a serving dish. Decorate with chocolate shavings and serve.

Mini-Meringues with Fresh Berries and Crème Fraîche

MINIPAVLOVA ZE ŚWIEŻYMI OWOCAMI

Serves 6 to 12 (makes twelve 3-in/7.5-cm meringues)

Qchnia Artystyczna—founded by cookery writer Marta Gessler in 1992, just after the fall of communism—was one of the first Warsaw restaurants to break new ground, both aesthetically and culinarily. Qchnia is located in the back of the Ujazdowski Castle, a somber, massive eighteenth-century building, which is the incongruous home of Warsaw's Centre for Contemporary Art. (And yes, the name looks as odd in Polish as in English: Qchnia is a deliberate misspelling of *kuchnia*, which means "kitchen.") Though it started life as a museum cafe, Qchnia's hip, unusual, and frequently changing decor has attracted a dedicated clientele. Qchnia often mixes and matches recipes, as a result of which you can eat Polish herring and Greek tzatziki in a single meal. Best of all, the restaurant has a fantastic terrace, with views over the Vistula River. It is the perfect place to sit on a hot day.

All of this is by way of providing background to this recipe for mini-Pavlovas. It is inspired by one of Gessler's, and it fits very much into her quirky aesthetic. A real Pavlova—meringue, cream, and fruit—is a somewhat pompous, cake-size creation. These individual Pavlovas are meant to be served one or two to a plate, so that each person gets her very own. You should use whatever fruit is in season: strawberries, blueberries, raspberries, cherries. Gessler calls for crème fraîche instead of whipped cream, which adds a sophisticated tartness to offset the sweetness of the meringue and berries.

FOR THE MERINGUES

4 egg whites, at room temperature

1 tsp vanilla extract

⅛ tsp cream of tartar

**1 cup/100 g sifted confectioners' sugar,
or 1 cup/225 g minus 1 tbsp superfine sugar**

FOR THE FILLING

2 cups/280 g fresh mixed berries, depending on what is in season (raspberries, blueberries, and/or quartered strawberries; sliced kiwi works here, too) or 1 cup/155 g pitted fresh cherries, if in season

1 tbsp sugar

¾ cup/180 ml crème fraîche or whipped cream

2 tbsp vanilla sugar, or 2 tbps white sugar plus 2 tsp vanilla extract

Handful of chopped fresh mint for garnish (optional)

TO MAKE THE MERINGUES: Preheat the oven to 225°F/110°C/gas ¼. Line a baking sheet with parchment paper.

In a large bowl, beat the egg whites until foamy using an electric mixer on medium-low speed. Beat in the vanilla and cream of tartar. Raise the speed to medium-high and beat in the confectioners' sugar, 1 tsp at a time. You want the sugar to be fully dissolved by the end. Beat until the mixture forms stiff peaks, but do not overbeat.

Dollop the mixture into mounds, about 2 tbsp per mound, on the prepared baking sheet, spacing them about 2 in/5 cm apart. You do not have to worry about being too fancy here with the shape, as the meringues will be heaped with fruit and cream. Flatten the mounds slightly so they can eventually accommodate the topping.

Bake for about 1 hour. You don't want the meringues to brown. They should be a little squishy when ready, but not soft. You can rotate the pan from front to back halfway through to ensure even baking, but don't open the oven door at all during the first 30 minutes. Turn the oven off when done, and rack the door open. Let the meringues cool inside the oven for at least 2 hours, or even overnight. (The meringues can be covered and stored at room temperature for several days.)

TO MAKE THE FILLING: Toss the berries (but not the cherries) with the sugar and refrigerate for at least 1 hour (or even overnight), so they have time to macerate and form a syrup. If you are using the cherries, whizz them in a food processor until smooth. (This is your cherry "sauce.")

Mix together the crème fraîche (or whipped cream) and vanilla sugar.

When the meringues are ready, set them upon a platter or individual plates. Dollop each one with the cream, and dribble the fresh berries over them. Add a spoonful or two of the cherry sauce, and sprinkle with mint, if you are using. Serve immediately.

Spicy Oranges

PIKANTNE POMARANCZE

Serves 6 to 8

Anne was first served this dessert at the home of Polish friends, who explained that it was Turkish. They had just been to Turkey and had fallen in love with the food—as had their ancestors before them. Turkish influences on Polish food, and on Polish style, go back a long way. Strange though it may sound today, the borders of the Polish-Lithuanian Commonwealth once stretched all the way to the borders of the Ottoman Empire. A long time ago, Anne visited the extraordinary Choćim fortress, built by Genoese architects in the thirteenth century, which once stood on the Polish-Turkish border. It now stands in central Ukraine.

The Poles fought the Turks many times in the sixteenth and seventeenth centuries, culminating in King Jan Sobieski III's triumph over the Turkish armies outside the gates of Vienna in 1683. That was the end of the Ottoman attempt to conquer Europe—hence the large painting of this victory that hangs in the Vatican, placed there by Pope John Paul II—and it was also the beginning of the end of the Polish-Lithuanian Commonwealth, which began to decline after Sobieski's death.

During those years of constant struggle, Turkish customs definitely rubbed off on the Poles. Over time, the Polish aristocracy adopted a version of Turkish dress—tunic, boots, shaved heads—which made them look very exotic in Western European courts. They also began to decorate the walls and floors of their chilly castles with Turkish carpets. Through the nineteenth and twentieth centuries, it was very common for Polish gentry to hang carpets over a fireplace or a sofa, as a backdrop for a pair of crossed swords. There is one over the mantelpiece at Chobielin.

Despite being Turkish, this recipe in fact fits well into the tradition of fresh and stewed spicy fruit desserts that are common in Poland, and that—who knows—may have come originally from Turkey four hundred years ago.

1½ cups/360 ml water

½ cup/115 g sugar

2 tbsp peeled and minced fresh ginger

4 to 5 cardamom pods, or 1 tsp ground cardamom

2 to 3 cinnamon sticks, or 1 tsp ground cinnamon

4 to 5 whole cloves

6 to 8 blood and navel oranges, in various shades of color if you can get them

2 tbsp candied orange peel, chopped

Ground cinnamon for sprinkling

In a small saucepan, bring the water to a boil. Add the sugar and spices. Boil over high heat until the sugar is dissolved, about 10 minutes. Remove from the heat and let steep for at least 30 minutes. Strain the syrup through a strainer and set aside.

In the meantime, slice the oranges thinly, but not so thinly that the slices fall apart. Cut around the edges to remove peel and pith. Arrange the slices on a serving platter. Pour the syrup over the oranges and chill in the refrigerator for at least 1 hour. When serving, sprinkle with the candied orange peel and a little cinnamon.

Red Fruit Salad

CZERWONA SAŁATKA OWOCOWA

Serves 6 to 8

Neither of us grew up eating red currants, and when Anne's red currant bushes first began to produce mountains of fruit at Chobielin, she wasn't quite sure what to do with them. She knew they could be used for excellent jams and jellies, and she discovered that they could also be put through a juicer to produce an amazingly refreshing summer drink, very close to lemonade but more sour.

Anne knew, too, that one can cook game with currants—but she wondered, was it really not possible to eat them fresh? They do have tiny pits, which can't be removed, and they are very sour. Eventually Anne discovered that if you toss them in a fruit salad with other sweet red fruits—such as raspberries and strawberries—and add sugar and a touch of liqueur, the edge of the sourness is taken off, and the pits somehow evaporate into the juiciness, adding only a mysterious crunch. This makes a light and beautiful summer dessert, and is particularly refreshing on a hot day.

> 2 cups/250 g fresh raspberries
>
> 2 cups/300 g fresh strawberries, hulled and quartered
>
> ½ cup/60 g fresh red currants or defrosted frozen red currants or preserved red currants, drained
>
> ½ cup/15 g chopped fresh mint
>
> ¼ cup/55 g sugar, plus more if needed
>
> 2 tbsp orange liqueur (Cointreau, Triple Sec, or Grand Marnier), plus more if needed

Toss all of the ingredients together in a serving bowl. Cover and refrigerate for 30 minutes or so, until the fruit has developed a nice syrupy coating. Test and add more liqueur, or more sugar, to taste. Serve immediately.

CHAPTER SEVEN

From a Polish Larder

Homemade Pickles
OGÓRKI KISZONE
page 260

Fresh Sour Pickles
KISZONE OGÓRKI
page 263

Preserved Dill Pickles in the Warsaw Style
OGÓRKI KONSERWOWE PO WARSZAWSKU
page 264

Plum Jam
POWIDŁA
page 265

Raspberry Cognac Jam
DŻEM MALINOWY Z KONIAKEM
page 268

Refreshing Mint Cordial
SOK MIĘTOWY
page 270

Infused Vodkas
NALEWKI
page 271

Cherry Vodka
WIŚNIÓWKA
page 272

Honey and Ginger–Spiced Vodka
NALEWKA MIODOWO-IMBIROWA
page 274

Orange-Rosemary Vodka
NALEWKA POMARAŃCZOWO-ROZMARYNOWA
page 275

Spicy Lithuanian Vodka
KRUPNIK LITEWSKI
page 276

Juniper Vodka
JAŁOWCÓWKA
page 277

Hot Mead
MIÓD PITNY NA CIEPŁO
page 279

Homemade Pickles

OGÓRKI KISZONE

If you've ever grown cucumbers in a garden and suddenly found yourself, 'round about mid-August, with hundreds of them, then you understand the origin of the dill pickle. Once you've made cucumber soup and cucumber salad every day for a week running, you need an alternative—and this is it. Besides, a fresh pickle— sold out of barrels in even the smallest Polish shops—is a delight on its own. And it is a staple ingredient in Polish cooking.

We include here two types of pickles. This first version—the fresh pickle—isn't one that many Americans know, unless they are lucky enough to have a delicatessen with a pickle barrel nearby. These crunchy pickles are not for keeping. Although they mature very quickly, and will taste good after only three days, they usually last for only a week or two. After that, they may begin to go soft.

If you want to make pickles that can be kept in your larder, to be eaten next week or next winter, then preserved pickles—the second version—is a better bet.

continued

Fresh Sour Pickles
KISZONE OGÓRKI

Makes about one 3-qt/2.8-L jar of pickles

Fresh pickles are best made in a wide-mouth ceramic container or glass jar that holds about 3 qt/2.8 L, preferably one with some sort of concave top that presses the pickles into the water. If you haven't got such a top—in fact we haven't—the traditional solution is to use a saucer. You put the saucer on top of the pickles, then you put a large stone or another heavy object on top of that.

This recipe is lower in salt than some (in case your diet requires you to reduce salt intake).

> **About 3 lb/1.4 kg small pickling cucumbers, or however many will fit in your jar**
> **4 garlic cloves, peeled**
> **2 pieces fresh horseradish root, each about 2 in/5 cm long**
> **The flowering top of an overgrown dill plant; or**
> **1 large bunch fresh dill, divided into 2 bundles and tied**
> **(The effect of the bundles is not quite as beautiful.)**
> **2 tbsp sea salt**

Place the cucumbers, garlic, horseradish, and dill in the jar (if you are using a dill plant, just bend it so it fits in). Sprinkle the salt on top. Pour in enough water to cover the pickles. Place a saucer on top, and then a weight on the saucer, so that the pickles are pressed down into the water. Leave somewhere cool for 3 days. There is no need to refrigerate. If a bit of mold or foam forms on the surface, scrape it off. The pickles should last for at least 1 week, and up to 1 month if you are lucky.

Preserved Dill Pickles in the Warsaw Style
OGÓRKI KONSERWOWE PO WARSZAWSKU

Makes about two 1-qt/960-ml jars of pickles

These are sweeter than the fresh pickles (see page 263), but not cloyingly so—unlike the jarred kind labeled "sweet" that you buy in the supermarket. These have just a whiff of sweetness. But if you don't like any sweetness at all, you can simply omit the sugar, bearing in mind that the pickles will not be considered "in the Warsaw style."

> 2¼ lb/1 kg pickling cucumbers
> 4 pieces horseradish root, each about 2 in/5 cm long
> 2 bay leaves
> 10 allspice berries
> ¾ cup/170 g sugar
> 2 cups/480 ml white wine vinegar
> 1 tsp sea salt
> The flowering top of an overgrown dill plant; or 1 large bunch
> fresh dill, divided into 2 bundles and tied (The effect of the
> bundles is not quite as lovely.)

Put two wide-mouth 1-qt/960-ml canning jars in a pot of boiling water to sterilize them. (You can also run them through the dishwasher.) Let cool.

Divide the cucumbers between the jars. In each jar place 2 pieces of the horseradish root, 1 bay leaf, 5 allspice berries, ¼ cup plus 2 tbsp/85 g sugar, 1 cup/240 ml white wine vinegar, and ½ tsp salt. Divide the dill flower in half and place a half in each jar. Fill the jars up to the top with water, wipe the rims, and seal tightly.

Place both jars in a large soup or pasta pot, and fill the pot with water, so that it covers about seven-eighths of each jar. The jar lids should not be submerged underwater. Bring the water to the boil, and continue boiling for 10 minutes. Remove the jars from the pot, cool, and store somewhere dark, such as a cupboard or cellar.

These pickles will be ready to eat after 3 months, and will last for 1 year or more.

VARIATION: *Add about 10 peeled garlic cloves to each jar (with or without the sugar), for a delicious garlicky pickle.*

Plum Jam

POWIDŁA

Makes six to eight 1-cup/240-ml jars of jam

Not all Polish jams rise to the level of striking originality. Strawberry jam is made in many countries, as are black currant jam and apricot jam, all of which Anne has made at Chobielin. *Powidła*, or plum jam, is different. It is not as runny as most English or American jams, and has a thick consistency, more akin to apple butter. When you stick a spoon into the jar, it doesn't fall over.

Powidła has a role in Polish cooking above and beyond that of ordinary jam. You can use it to cook pork, or add it to a sauce instead of sugar. It is also, somehow, the perfect thing to spread on *naleśniki*, Polish pancakes (see page 221). It isn't difficult, but it does require quite a long cooking time. The point here is to boil all of the water out of the plums, reducing them to their gooey, sticky, delicious essence. It's an excellent thing to do if you are hanging around the house one day. But even if you have to go out suddenly, it doesn't matter. Turn off the burner, and then turn it on again when you get home.

The plums that Poles always use for this jam are called *węgierki*, which means "little Hungarians," a name that is presumably a clue to their origin. Anne has several trees that produce *węgierki*, though irregularly; some years she has so many that she makes enough *powidła* to last a decade. In other years, there are none at all (and then Anne's family eats the *powidła* made the year before). In English, *węgierki* are known as "damsons." Other cooking plums can be substituted, but really juicy plums may not produce the thick jam that you want.

> **4½ lb/2 kg very ripe cooking plums**
> **About 2¼ cups/505 g sugar (You may not need all of it.)**

Put six to eight 1-cup/240-ml jam jars in a pot of boiling water to sterilize them. (You can also run them through the dishwasher.) Let cool.

Prepare the plums by cutting each one open and removing the pit. If they are ripe enough, the pits should slip right out. There is no need to cut them further.

Pour the plums into a large soup or stew pot, and bring to a simmer over low heat. They will need to simmer, we're afraid, for the whole day—8 hours minimum, but 10 is better. As noted above, this can be done with interruptions, 4 hours here, 4 hours there. The cooking time will vary slightly, depending on the ripeness of your plums: Very juicy ones will take longer, drier plums will be finished more quickly. Stir occasionally, and of course make sure the plums do not burn. Do not add water since, as noted, the point is to eliminate the water.

continued

About 1 hour before the plums are done cooking, add half of the sugar. Mix it into the plums, and taste—this is very important. If your plums are very sweet, you might not need to add any more sugar. If not, add the rest now. We use very little sugar in our *powidła*, because we don't like very sweet jam, but we recognize that this is a matter of personal taste. Continue simmering. When the *powidła* is done, it should be very thick, and not at all runny. If there is any liquid left at all, it needs to be simmered longer.

Pour the jam into the sterilized jars, wipe the rims, and seal tightly. Place the jars in a pot, fill the pot with water so that it covers each jar by about 2 in/5 cm of water, and bring to a boil. Let the water boil for 10 minutes.

Remove the jars from the pot, cool, and store.

Raspberry Cognac Jam

DŻEM MALINOWY Z KONIAKEM

Makes six to eight 1-cup/240-ml jars of jam

After *Powidła* (page 265), there is one other jam whose authentically Polish origins we would be willing to defend, and it is this one. In one Polish cookbook, Anne found a version of this called "Raspberry Jam for Real Men," though we think women will like it, too. This has a more sophisticated flavor than ordinary raspberry jam. It can be used in much the same way—spread on breakfast toast, for example—but adds a more adult twist. Serve this on *naleśniki*, or Polish pancakes (see page 221), and it makes for an interesting, more grown-up dessert.

>4½ cups/555 g ripe fresh raspberries
>6¼ cups/1.4 kg sugar
>Juice of 1 large lemon
>3 cups plus 2 tbsp/750 ml Cognac or another brandy

Put six to eight 1-cup/240-ml jam jars in a pot of boiling water to sterilize them. (You can also run them through the dishwasher.) Let cool.

Place the raspberries in a large pot. Mix in the sugar and let sit for 2 to 3 hours, until the berries begin giving off their juice. Add the lemon juice and bring to a boil, stirring. Lower the heat and simmer, stirring constantly, for about 10 minutes, until thickened to a more jamlike consistency. Remove from the heat and let cool.

Do this one more time—bring the jam to a boil and simmer, stirring constantly, for 10 minutes, or until the jam is the consistency you desire. Remove from the heat. Slowly pour in the Cognac, mixing constantly.

While still hot, pour the jam into the sterilized jars, wipe the rims, and seal tightly. Place the jars in a pot, fill the pot so the water covers the jar by at least 2 in/5 cm, and bring to a boil. Let the water boil for 10 minutes.

Remove the jars from the pot, cool, and store.

Refreshing Mint Cordial

SOK MIĘTOWY

Serves 4 to 8, depending on how thirsty everyone is

Like many other recipes in this book, this one arose from abundance: One summer, half of Anne's vegetable garden seemed to be overrun with mint, and she had to find something to do with it. And like so many others, she has always looked for cold, refreshing things to drink in the summer that aren't soda or canned juices. Traditional Polish cooking was a great place to search, because until remarkably recently there wasn't much in the way of soda or canned juice available.

On a hot day, drink this cordial instead of iced tea or lemonade, and make sure you sit in the shade while doing so.

> 2 cups/480 ml water
> 2 tbsp dried mint leaves
> 2 cups/480 ml apple juice, fresh if possible, or a high-quality store-bought brand, not too sweet
> 1 tsp fresh lemon juice
> 1 tsp honey
> Fresh mint leaves for garnish

In a medium saucepan, bring the water to a boil, and throw in the dried mint. Reduce the heat to very low, cover, and simmer slowly for 30 minutes.

Remove from the heat, add the apple juice, lemon juice, and honey and mix well. Pour into bottles, cap or cork, and keep upright in a cool, dark place for 2 to 3 days. The mint will sink to the bottom of the bottles. If you want, strain before serving.

Serve chilled, with fresh mint leaves for garnish.

Infused Vodkas

NALEWKI

The creation of flavored vodka is an art as ancient as the production of alcohol itself. In essence, it is simple to the point of banality. Cut up some fruit, maybe add some spices. Pour pure alcohol over the mixture. Leave the jar in a dark place for a couple of weeks, or up to 6 months. Drink—sparingly, of course.

In practice, however, there are a few tricks to know. Vodka can be flavored simply, infused with lemon or honey. It can also be infused with more exotic ingredients, such as ginger or pomegranate. One traditional Polish recipe for *Starka*, also very ancient, adds brandy to the mix. Another, *Żubrówka*, is flavored with bison grass, a plant that grows in the eastern part of the country. Bison grass, as its name indicates, is the grass supposedly most favored by Europe's last living bison, which inhabit the Białowieża Forest between Poland and Belarus. The Ukrainians use hot red peppers to make Pertsovka, which we find spicy to the point of being undrinkable. In a Carpathian village, Anne was once given rose-flavored vodka made from rosehips, which she found spectacular.

The most important starting point is, of course, the vodka itself. The quality matters. Though in essence, it is a drink made from rotten potatoes, the amount of filtering and distillation makes a big difference. (Quick hint: If it smells like rubbing alcohol, then pour it down the drain.) There are some acceptable Polish brands—Belvedere, Chopin, or Wyborowa—and of course there is Swedish Absolut and Russian Stolichnaya (though the latter comes in varying degrees of drinkability, so beware).

The second important element is the ingredients, which must be fresh, not dried or frozen. Fruit has to be very ripe, not green. Spices, such as ginger or nutmeg, are best if used the instant they are cut or ground.

As for what you make the vodka in, the only thing that matters is that the bottle has an airtight lid. You can buy expensive infusion bottles, which have a spigot at the bottom. You can also make large quantities in gooseneck bottles, which can be purchased in Polish supermarkets. But there is no reason not to use a large kitchen jar. You can then pour the infused vodka into fancy corked bottles (easily purchased on the Internet or at kitchen stores), which will look very exotic on your drinks tray. They also make terrific Christmas presents.

continued

Cherry Vodka
WIŚNIÓWKA

Makes one 34-oz/1-L bottle of vodka

"Life is dandy, cherry brandy!" So goes a line from a poem by Russian writer Osip Mandelstam—meant to be ironic, of course, as he lived in the darkest days of Stalinism and died in the Gulag. Cherry brandy, cherry vodka, cherry liqueurs: These are the obvious consequence of Eastern Europe's famous and abundant cherry orchards, of which there are just as many in Poland as there are in provincial Russia. Do note that this recipe works for any kind of fruit that is not too sweet. In particular it is worth trying with black currants or Polish *jagody*—wild blueberries—if you can find them.

The quantities given here are for a 34-oz/1-L jar, but do reduce them (or increase them!) in proportion to the bottle you are using.

> 1⅛ lb/510 g fresh sour cherries (or black currants or *jagody*)
> 25 oz/750 ml clear vodka
> 1 to 2 tbsp sugar (optional)

Pit and halve the cherries. As in all vodka recipes, it is important that the flesh of the fruit be somehow exposed.

Fill a jar with the cherries, but do not pack it. Pour the vodka on top and seal tightly. Leave in a dark place, preferably for at least 2 weeks—or up to 6 months. At the end of that time, open the jar and strain. If you have a very-fine-mesh strainer, that will do. If not, use an ordinary strainer lined with a cheesecloth or even a coffee filter. Set the strainer over a large bowl, ideally one from which you'll be able to easily pour afterward. Pour the vodka mixture through the strainer and allow the fruit to sit, seeping liquid, for a good hour or so, stirring a bit and pressing if need be to make the liquid go through.

Now taste the vodka. Add sugar if you want an after-dinner liqueur, or leave it out if you want something sharper. Pour (or ladle) into a decorative bottle.

Honey and Ginger–Spiced Vodka
NALEWKA MIODOWO-IMBIROWA

Makes one 34-oz/1-L bottle of vodka

4 to 5 thick slices peeled fresh ginger
1 cinnamon stick
½ vanilla bean pod (about 1½ in/1.25 cm)
1 whole nutmeg
6 whole cloves
4 juniper berries
2 cups/480 ml water
1 cup/240 ml honey
25 oz/750 ml clear vodka

Place the ginger, cinnamon stick, vanilla bean pod, nutmeg, cloves, juniper berries, and 1 cup/240 ml of the water in a saucepan and bring to a boil. Remove from the heat and let cool.

Meanwhile, place the honey in a separate saucepan, add the remaining 1 cup/240 ml water, and bring to a boil. Skim off any foam from the top and remove from the heat. Let cool.

Pour both liquids into a jar, add the vodka, and seal tightly. Let sit in a dark place for at least 2 weeks or up to 6 months. Strain through a fine-mesh strainer or a regular strainer lined with a coffee filter or cheesecloth, and discard the spices.

Pour into a decorative bottle.

Orange-Rosemary Vodka

NALEWKA POMARAŃCZOWO-ROZMARYNOWA

Makes one 34-oz/1-L bottle of vodka

**2 large navel oranges, halved and peeled,
with as much pith removed as possible**

2 cups/480 ml water

Handful of fresh rosemary, stems removed

25 oz/750 ml clear vodka

1 to 2 tbsp sugar

Combine the oranges, water, and rosemary in a saucepan and bring to a boil.
Continue boiling for 1 minute, and then remove from the heat and let cool.
Pour into a jar, add the vodka, and seal tightly. Leave in a dark place for at least
2 weeks or up to 6 months. Strain through a fine-mesh strainer or a regular
strainer lined with a coffee filter or cheesecloth, and discard the oranges and
rosemary. Add the sugar, if desired.

Pour into a decorative bottle.

Spicy Lithuanian Vodka
KRUPNIK LITEWSKI

Makes one 34-oz/1-L bottle of vodka

This is the traditional recipe, and we fear it contains some unusual ingredients, namely dried rose hips and rue, which you might be able to buy at a specialty store but are better off growing in your garden. If you can't find rue, substitute a few grinds of pepper, and if you can't find rose hips, don't worry about it.

> 1 cup/240 ml boiled and cooled water
> 1 cup/240 ml dark-colored honey
> 1 cup/225 g sugar
> 2 cinnamon sticks
> 1 small whole nutmeg
> 1 tbsp dried rose hips (optional)
> 12 whole cloves
> 2 juniper berries
> 5 to 7 sprigs rue (or a few grinds of pepper)
> 25 oz/750 ml clear vodka

In a large soup pot, combine everything but the vodka and bring to a boil. Cover, reduce the heat, and cook at a low boil for 10 to 15 minutes. Remove from the heat and slowly pour in the vodka. Put back on the burner and warm up the mixture on low heat. Do not boil.

You can, if you want, filter this through a cheesecloth-lined strainer or a strainer with very fine mesh and then drink immediately. Alternatively, you can cover and let cool overnight. Then filter and pour into a bottle. Seal the bottle and leave for 2 to 3 months in a dark place.

Then drink, sitting by the fire. You can sip it cold, or heat it up like a *vin chaud* (hot wine).

Juniper Vodka
JAŁOWCÓWKA

Makes one 34-oz/1-L bottle of vodka

Angelica root, which can be used in this recipe, is sometimes an ingredient in Scotch whisky. Again, if you can't find it, just leave it out.

¼ cup/55 g juniper berries
1 tbsp allspice berries
3 cinnamon sticks
2 tbsp freshly grated orange zest
1 large piece angelica root (optional)
25 oz/750 ml clear vodka
8 cups/2 L water
½ cup/115 g sugar

Place all of the spices and the orange zest in a jar (and angelica root, if using), pour the vodka on top, and seal tightly. Store for at least 2 weeks in a dark place. Strain through a fine-mesh strainer or a regular strainer lined with a coffee filter or cheesecloth.

In a medium saucepan over medium heat, mix the water and sugar and boil gently, stirring until the sugar is completely dissolved. Let cool and mix with the vodka. Pour into a bottle with a cork or tight seal, seal the bottles, and leave in a dark place again for at least 2 weeks.

Open the bottles and filter again. Reseal the bottles and leave in a cold, dark place for 6 to 8 months. The longer you leave them, the better the vodka will taste.

Hot Mead

MIÓD PITNY NA CIEPŁO

Serves 4 to 6 (makes about 20 oz/600 ml)

Mead—fermented honey—is a Polish drink that goes back to the Middle Ages. In Polish sagas and epics, warriors drink mead before battles. Even now it has an indefinable, and probably undeserved, reputation as a healthier form of alcohol. In Poland you can buy bottled mead, the making of which grows more sophisticated every year. At a dinner organized in Warsaw not long ago by Slow Food Polska—the Polish branch of the international Slow Food movement—Anne was served several extraordinary organic meads, each made by a slightly different method. The company that produces them, Pasieka Jaros, has been researching and experimenting with ancient methods of mead production for more than thirty years.

This recipe is something slightly different: It's a hot form of Honey and Ginger Spiced–Vodka (page 274), which you can make at home. Serve this as a winter cocktail—or after a day spent cross-country skiing—and drink it in front of a roaring fire.

½ cup/120 ml honey
1 cup/240 ml water
3 to 4 cloves
6 cinnamon sticks
1 whole vanilla bean pod (about 3 in/7.5 cm long)
One 1-in/2.5-cm strip orange rind
1 small chunk from a whole nutmeg, or ¼ tsp ground
16 oz/480 ml vodka

In a medium saucepan, bring the honey and water to a boil, skimming any foam from the surface. Add the cloves, cinnamon sticks, vanilla bean pod, and orange rind, return to a boil, and remove from the heat. Let sit for 1 or 2 minutes, then bring to a boil again. Remove from the heat, cover, and set aside for at least 30 minutes to steep. Strain through a fine-mesh strainer or a regular strainer lined with a coffee filter or cheesecloth, and again bring to a boil. Pour in the vodka. Stir well and serve piping hot.

Index

A

Almonds
    Chicken Salad with Arugula, 150–52
    Chocolate Mazurek, 248–49
    Orange and Almond Mazurek, 247
    Poppy-Seed Torte, 242–44

Apples
    Apple Latkes, 218
    Beet, Apple, and Horseradish Salad, 99
    Celery Root and Green Apple Salad, 98
    Easy Microwave Applesauce, 220
    Herring with Lime and Raspberries, 50
    Herring with Sour Cream and Apples, 49
    Roasted Beets for Game, 122

Arugula
    Chicken Salad with Arugula, 150–52
    Sorrel Soup, 75–76

B

Babka rumowa, 234–35

Bacon
    Hunter's Stew, 184–87
    Potato, Cheese, Bacon, and Peas Filling for Pierogi, 207–8
    Sour Bread Soup, 78–79

Barley
    Traditional Zupa Grzybowa, 71

Barlik, Roman, 176

Barszcz, 63–65

Barszcz biały, 78–79

Beans
    Green or Yellow Beans à la Polonaise, 108–9
    New Potato and Yellow Bean Salad, 106

Beef
    Beef Tenderloin with Wild Mushrooms and Dill Pickle, 172–73
    Hunter's Stew, 184–87
    Steak Tartare, 53–55
    Stewed Beef Rolls with Kasha, 169–70
    Traditional Barszcz, 64

Beets
    Beet, Apple, and Horseradish Salad, 99
    Beet, Cherry, and Garlic Salad, 100
    A Jazzier Barszcz, 65
    peeling, 63
    Roasted Beets for Game, 122
    Summer Beet Soup, 67–68
    Traditional Barszcz, 64
    Winter Roasted Beet Salad, 110

Befszyk tatarski, 53–55

Berries. *See also individual berries*
    Mini-Meringues with Fresh Berries and Crème Fraîche, 250–51
    Red Fruit Salad, 255

Beverages
    Cherry Vodka, 272
    Honey and Ginger–Spiced Vodka, 274
    Hot Mead, 279
    Juniper Vodka, 277
    Orange-Rosemary Vodka, 275
    Refreshing Mint Cordial, 270
    Spicy Lithuanian Vodka, 276

Bielik-Robson, Agata, 48

Bigos, 184–87

Blini and Caviar, 42–45

Bliny z kawiorem, 42–45

Boar, wild, 193
    Roast Loin of Wild Boar with Sour Cherries, 193–95

A Boozier Zupa Grzybowa, 72–73

Braised Cabbage with Wine and Nutmeg, 118

Bread Soup, Sour, 78–79

Buraki do podania z dziczyzną, 122

Butter Lettuce and Endive Salad, 103

C

Cabbage
  Braised Cabbage with Wine and
  Nutmeg, 118
  Cabbage Rolls with Meat Stuffing and
  Wild Mushroom Sauce, 142–44
  Cabbage Rolls with Wild Mushroom
  Stuffing in Tomato Broth, 140–41
  Classic Coleslaw, 102
  Duck and Red Cabbage Filling with
  Orange Butter for Pierogi, 211–13
  Hunter's Stew, 184–87
  Red Cabbage with Cranberries, 117
Cakes. *See also Mazurki*
  Cheesecake with Strawberry–Red
  Currant Sauce, 239–41
  Gingerbread Cake, 231–32
  Lithuanian Honey Cake, 236–37
  Orange-Saffron Rum Cake, 234–35
  Plum Cake, 233
  Poppy-Seed Torte, 242–44
Carrots
  Chicken Blanquette Polonaise, 153–55
  Garlicky Carrots and Zucchini, 111
  Roasted Winter Vegetables, 120
Caviar
  Caviar and Blini, 42–45
  Eggplant Caviar, 46–47
  history of, 42, 44
  Salmon Fillets with Caviar, 135–37
  types of, 44, 135
Celery root
  Celery Root and Green Apple Salad, 98
  Celery Root Pâté, 125
  Chicken Blanquette Polonaise, 153–55
  Mashed Potatoes with Celery Root,
  123
  Purée of Celery Root and Sunchokes,
  124
  Roasted Winter Vegetables, 120
Cheese
  Cheesecake with Strawberry–Red
  Currant Sauce, 239–41
  Potato, Cheese, Bacon, and Peas
  Filling for Pierogi, 207–8
  Truffles and Brown Butter Filling for
  Pierogi, 209

Cherries
  Beet, Cherry, and Garlic Salad, 100
  Cherry Vodka, 272
  Mini-Meringues with Fresh Berries
  and Crème Fraîche, 250–51
  Roast Loin of Wild Boar with Sour
  Cherries, 193–95
Chestnut-Potato Mash, Rich Turkey
Patties in Madeira Sauce with, 166–68
Chicken
  Cabbage Rolls with Meat Stuffing and
  Wild Mushroom Sauce, 142–44
  Chicken Blanquette Polonaise, 153–55
  Chicken Breasts with Chanterelle
  Sauce, 145–47
  Chicken-in-a-Pot, 161–63
  Chicken Salad with Arugula, 150–52
  Chicken Soup, 80–83
  Roast Chicken with Clementines,
  158–60
  Stuffed Chicken Breasts with Cognac
  Sauce, 148–49
  Weeknight Roast Chicken, 156–57
Chłodnik, 67–68
Chocolate Mazurek, 248–49
Ciecierska, Iwona, 88
Ciecierski, Tomasz, 88
Classic Coleslaw, 102
Clementines, Roast Chicken with, 158–60
Cognac
  Raspberry Cognac Jam, 268
  Stuffed Chicken Breasts with Cognac
  Sauce, 148–49
Coleslaw, Classic, 102
Comber sarni z suszonymi śliwkami, 180–81
Cookies, Gingerbread, 228–30
Cranberries, Red Cabbage with, 117
Cucumbers
  Fresh Sour Pickles, 263
  Grandpa Ben's Cucumber Salad, 104
  Preserved Dill Pickles in the Warsaw
  Style, 264
  Sour Cucumber Soup, 60–61
  Summer Beet Soup, 67–68
Currants
  Cheesecake with Strawberry–Red
  Currant Sauce, 239–41
  Red Fruit Salad, 255

Czerwona kapusta żurawiną, 117

Czerwona sałatka owocowa, 255

Czosnkowa marchewka i cukinia, 111

D

Dates
  Venison Stew, 182–83

Desserts
  Cheesecake with Strawberry–Red Currant Sauce, 239–41
  Chocolate Mazurek, 248–49
  Gingerbread Cake, 231–32
  Gingerbread Cookies, 228–30
  Lithuanian Honey Cake, 236–37
  Mini-Meringues with Fresh Berries and Crème Fraîche, 250–51
  Orange and Almond Mazurek, 247
  Orange-Saffron Rum Cake, 234–35
  Plum Cake, 233
  Poppy-Seed Torte, 242–44
  Spicy Oranges, 252–53

Dill, 106

Dripped Noodles, 86

Duck
  Duck and Red Cabbage Filling with Orange Butter for Pierogi, 211–13
  Duck Breast with Sautéed Pears and Shallots, 164–65

Dumplings. *See* Pierogi

Dżem malinowy z koniakem, 268

E

Easy Microwave Applesauce, 220

Eggplant Caviar, 46–47

Endive and Butter Lettuce Salad, 103

F

Fasolka szparagowa (zielona albo zolta) à la polonaise, 108–9

Fasolka z ziemniakami, 106

Femme Fatale, 239

Fennel
  Venison Stew, 182–83

Filety z łososia z kawiorem, 135–37

Filety z pstrąga w sosie cytrynowym, 131

Fish
  Herring with Lime and Raspberries, 50
  Herring with Sour Cream and Apples, 49
  Salmon Fillets with Caviar, 135–37
  Sturgeon Steaks with Hot Mustard, 132–34
  Trout with Lemon Cream Sauce, 131

Foolproof Matzoh Balls, 84–85

Fresh Sour Pickles, 263

Fruit. *See also individual fruits*
  pierogi, 214
    Red Fruit Salad, 255

Frum, Barbara, 84

G

Garlicky Carrots and Zucchini, 111

Gessler, Magda, 32

Gessler, Marta, 32, 111, 250

Ginger
  Gingerbread Cake, 231–32
  Gingerbread Cookies, 228–30
  Honey and Ginger–Spiced Vodka, 274
  Orange Filling with Ginger and Cointreau for Pierogi, 215

Gołąbki, 139–44

Grandpa Ben's Cucumber Salad, 104

Green or Yellow Beans à la Polonaise, 108–9

Grimes, Paul, 200

Grochówka, 90–91

Grzyby, 112–15

Gulasz z kurczaka, 153–55

Gulasz z sarniny, 182–83

Gurdon, Meghan, 234

H

Ham
  New Potato and Yellow Bean Salad, 106
  Split Pea Soup, 90–91

Herring
  Herring with Lime and Raspberries, 50
  Herring with Sour Cream and Apples, 49

serving, 48
shopping for, 48
Hirschowitz, Louis, 161
Honey
    Honey and Ginger–Spiced Vodka, 274
    Hot Mead, 279
    Lithuanian Honey Cake, 236–37
Hotel Europejski, 30, 53
Hotel Pod Orłem, 174
Hot Mead, 279
Hunter's Stew, 184–87

J

Jałowcówka, 277
Jams
    Plum Jam, 265–67
    Raspberry Cognac Jam, 268
A Jazzier Barszcz, 65
Jerzy, Rafał, 176
Jesiotr z sosem musztardowym, 132–34
Juniper Vodka, 277

K

Kachelska, Romka, 239
Kaczka z gruszkami, 164–65
Kasha, 171
    Stewed Beef Rolls with Kasha, 169–70
Kawior z bakłażana, 46–47
Kiszone ogórki, 263
Klimont-Bodzinska, Ola, 108
Klopsiki z indyka, 166–68
Knejdlach, 84–85
Koranyi, Noemi, 164
Kotlet schabowy, 188–89
Krupnik litewski, 276
Kurczak pieczony po polsku, 156–57
Kurczak pieczony z klementynkami, 158–60
Kurczak w sosie kurkowym, 145–47

L

Lane kluski, 86
Latkes, Apple, 218
Lawson, Nigella, 37, 65

Lemons
    Orange and Almond Mazurek, 247
    Trout with Lemon Cream Sauce, 131
Lettuce
    Butter Lettuce and Endive Salad, 103
    types of, 103
Lime, Herring with Raspberries and, 50
Lithuanian Honey Cake, 236–37
"Little Doves," 139–44
Liver with Caramelized Onions in Madeira Sauce, 174–75
Lukins, Sheila, 37
Luxe Turkey Patties with Fresh Truffles, 168

M

Madeira
    Liver with Caramelized Onions in Madeira Sauce, 174–75
    Rich Turkey Patties in Madeira Sauce with Potato-Chestnut Mash, 166–68
    Venison Stew, 182–83
Mandelstam, Osip, 272
Mashed Potatoes with Celery Root, 123
Master Pierogi Recipe, 202
Matzoh Balls, Foolproof, 84–85
Mazurek czekoladowy, 248–49
Mazurek pomarańczowy, 247
Mazurki, 245
    Chocolate Mazurek, 248–49
    Orange and Almond Mazurek, 247
Mead, Hot, 279
Mickiewicz, Adam, 169
Mini-Meringues with Fresh Berries and Crème Fraîche, 250–51
Minipavlova ze świeżymi owocami, 250–51
Mint Cordial, Refreshing, 270
Miódownik starolitewski, 236–37
Miód pitny na ciepło, 279
Mizeria dziadka Benjamina, 104
Mushrooms
    Beef Tenderloin with Wild Mushrooms and Dill Pickle, 172–73
    A Boozier Zupa Grzybowa, 72–73
    Cabbage Rolls with Meat Stuffing and Wild Mushroom Sauce, 142–44

Cabbage Rolls with Wild Mushroom Stuffing in Tomato Broth, 140–41

Chicken Blanquette Polonaise, 153–55

Chicken Breasts with Chanterelle Sauce, 145–47

cleaning, 115

drying, 115

gathering, 112

Hunter's Stew, 184–87

Stewed Beef Rolls with Kasha, 169–70

Stuffed Chicken Breasts with Cognac Sauce, 148–49

Traditional Zupa Grzybowa, 71

Turkey Patties with Mushrooms, 168

Twice-Cooked Wild Mushrooms, 112–15

types of, 114

Wild Mushrooms and Sauerkraut Filling for Pierogi, 210

Mustard Soup, 88–89

Mus u jabłkowy z mikrofalòwki, 220

N

Naleśniki, 221–23

Nalewka miodowo-imbirowa, 274

Nalewka pomarańczowo-rozmarynowa, 275

New Potato and Yellow Bean Salad, 106

Next-Day Tomato Soup, 87

Noodles

Dripped Noodles, 86

Next-Day Tomato Soup, 87

O

Ochorowicz-Monatowa, Marja, 35, 37

Ogórki konserwowe po Warszawsku, 264

Ogórkowa, 60–61

Onions, Caramelized, Liver with, in Madeira Sauce, 174–75

Oranges

Duck and Red Cabbage Filling with Orange Butter for Pierogi, 211–13

Orange and Almond Mazurek, 247

Orange Filling with Ginger and Cointreau for Pierogi, 215

Orange-Rosemary Vodka, 275

Orange-Saffron Rum Cake, 234–35

Roast Pork Tenderloin with Orange and Rosemary, 192

Spicy Oranges, 252–53

P

Pacholska, Pani, 71

Pancakes

Apple Latkes, 218

Rolled Pancakes with Jam, 221–23

Parsnips

Chicken Blanquette Polonaise, 153–55

Roasted Winter Vegetables, 120

Pasieka Jaros, 279

Pasztet z selera, 125

Pâté, Celery Root, 125

Pears, Sautéed, Duck Breast with Shallots and, 164–65

Peas

Potato, Cheese, Bacon, and Peas Filling for Pierogi, 207–8

Split Pea Soup, 90–91

Pickles, 260

Beef Tenderloin with Wild Mushrooms and Dill Pickle, 172–73

Fresh Sour Pickles, 263

Preserved Dill Pickles in the Warsaw Style, 264

Sour Cucumber Soup, 60–61

Pieczona dynia, 119

Pieczona warzywa, 120

Pierniczki, 228–30

Piernik, 231–32

Pierogi

Duck and Red Cabbage Filling with Orange Butter, 211–13

fruit, 214

history of, 200

Master Pierogi Recipe, 202

Orange Filling with Ginger and Cointreau, 215

Potato, Cheese, Bacon, and Peas Filling, 207–8

Strawberry Filling with Sour Cream and Brown Sugar, 217

Truffles and Brown Butter Filling, 209

Wild Mushrooms and Sauerkraut Filling, 210

Piersí kurczaka z farszem grzybowym,
148–49

Pikantne pomarancze, 252–53

Placek, 233

Placki z jabłkami, 218

Plums
    Plum Cake, 233
    Plum Jam, 265–67
    types of, 265

Polędwica wieprzowy w pomarańczach i rozmarynie, 192

Polędwica z dzika z wiśniami, 193–95

Polędwica z grzybami i kiszonymi ogórkami, 172–73

Polędwiczki sarnie, 179

Poppy-Seed Torte, 242–44

Pork
    Cabbage Rolls with Meat Stuffing and Wild Mushroom Sauce, 142–44
    Hunter's Stew, 184–87
    Pork Loin Stuffed with Prunes, 190–91
    Roast Loin of Wild Boar with Sour Cherries, 193–95
    Roast Pork Tenderloin with Orange and Rosemary, 192
    Wiener Schnitzel, Polish Style, 188–89

Potatoes
    Mashed Potatoes with Celery Root, 123
    New Potato and Yellow Bean Salad, 106
    Potato, Cheese, Bacon, and Peas Filling for Pierogi, 207–8
    Rich Turkey Patties in Madeira Sauce with Potato-Chestnut Mash, 166–68
    Sour Cucumber Soup, 60–61
    Truffles and Brown Butter Filling for Pierogi, 209

Potrawka z kurczaka, 161–63

Powidła, 265–67

Preserved Dill Pickles in the Warsaw Style, 264

Prunes
    Hunter's Stew, 184–87
    Pork Loin Stuffed with Prunes, 190–91

Rack of Venison with Prune Purée, 180–81

Puck, Wolfgang, 84

Pumpkin, Roasted, 119

Purée of Celery Root and Sunchokes, 124

Puré selera z topinamburam, 124

Q

Qchnia Artystyczna, 250

R

Rack of Venison with Prune Purée, 180–81

Raisins
    Cheesecake with Strawberry–Red Currant Sauce, 239–41
    Orange-Saffron Rum Cake, 234–35

Raspberries
    Herring with Lime and Raspberries, 50
    Raspberry Cognac Jam, 268
    Red Fruit Salad, 255

Red Cabbage with Cranberries, 117

Red Fruit Salad, 255

Refreshing Mint Cordial, 270

Restauracja 1921, 174

Rice
    Cabbage Rolls with Meat Stuffing and Wild Mushroom Sauce, 142–44
    Chicken-in-a-Pot, 161–63
    Next-Day Tomato Soup, 87

Rich Turkey Patties in Madeira Sauce with Potato-Chestnut Mash, 166–68

Roast Chicken with Clementines, 158–60

Roasted Beets for Game, 122

Roasted Pumpkin, 119

Roasted Winter Vegetables, 120

Roast Loin of Wild Boar with Sour Cherries, 193–95

Roast Pork Tenderloin with Orange and Rosemary, 192

Rolled Pancakes with Jam, 221–23

Rosoł, 80–83

Rosso, Julee, 37

Rum Cake, Orange-Saffron, 234–35

S

Salads
   Beet, Apple, and Horseradish Salad, 99
   Beet, Cherry, and Garlic Salad, 100
   Butter Lettuce and Endive Salad, 103
   Celery Root and Green Apple Salad, 98
   Chicken Salad with Arugula, 150–52
   Classic Coleslaw, 102
   Grandpa Ben's Cucumber Salad, 104
   New Potato and Yellow Bean Salad, 106
   Red Fruit Salad, 255
   Winter Roasted Beet Salad, 110
Sałatka z kapustą, 102
Sałatka z kurczaka z rukolą, 150–52
Sałatka z sałaty i cykorii, 103
Salmon Fillets with Caviar, 135–37
Sauerkraut
   Hunter's Stew, 184–87
   Wild Mushrooms and Sauerkraut Filling for Pierogi, 210
Sausage
   Hunter's Stew, 184–87
   Sour Bread Soup, 78–79
   Split Pea Soup, 90–91
Schab pieczony ze śliwkami, 190–91
Sernik z polewą z truskawek i czerwonych porzeczek, 239–41
Sikorski, Klemens, 176
Slow Food movement, 32, 279
Sok miętowy, 270
Sorrel Soup, 75–76
Soups
   A Boozier Zupa Grzybowa, 72–73
   Chicken Soup, 80–83
   A Jazzier Barszcz, 65
   Mustard Soup, 88–89
   Next-Day Tomato Soup, 87
   Sorrel Soup, 75–76
   Sour Bread Soup, 78–79
   Sour Cucumber Soup, 60–61
   Split Pea Soup, 90–91
   Summer Beet Soup, 67–68
   Traditional Barszcz, 64
   Traditional Zupa Grzybowa, 71
Sour Bread Soup, 78–79
Sour Cucumber Soup, 60–61
Spago, 84
Spicy Lithuanian Vodka, 276
Spicy Oranges, 252–53
Split Pea Soup, 90–91
Steak Tartare, 53–55
Stewed Beef Rolls with Kasha, 169–70
Stews
   Hunter's Stew, 184–87
   Venison Stew, 182–83
Strawberries
   Cheesecake with Strawberry–Red Currant Sauce, 239–41
   Red Fruit Salad, 255
   Strawberry Filling with Sour Cream and Brown Sugar for Pierogi, 217
Stuffed Chicken Breasts with Cognac Sauce, 148–49
Sturgeon Steaks with Hot Mustard, 132–34
Summer Beet Soup, 67–68
Sunchokes, Purée of Celery Root and, 124
Surówka, 97
Szemberg, Włodek, 60
Szymanderska, Hanna, 35, 86

T

Tomatoes
   Cabbage Rolls with Wild Mushroom Stuffing in Tomato Broth, 140–41
   Eggplant Caviar, 46–47
   Next-Day Tomato Soup, 87
Tort makowy, 242–44
Traditional Barszcz, 64
Traditional Zupa Grzybowa, 71
Trout with Lemon Cream Sauce, 131
Truffles
   Luxe Turkey Patties with Fresh Truffles, 168
   Truffles and Brown Butter Filling for Pierogi, 209

Turkey
    Luxe Turkey Patties with Fresh Truffles, 168
    Rich Turkey Patties in Madeira Sauce with Potato-Chestnut Mash, 166–68
    Turkey Patties with Mushrooms, 168
Twice-Cooked Wild Mushrooms, 112–15

U

U Kucharze, 53

V

Veal
    Hunter's Stew, 184–87
    Traditional Barszcz, 64
Vegetables. *See also individual vegetables*
    Roasted Winter Vegetables, 120
Venison, 176–77
    Hunter's Stew, 184–87
    Rack of Venison with Prune Purée, 180–81
    Venison Noisettes, 179
    Venison Stew, 182–83
Vodka
    Cherry Vodka, 272
    Honey and Ginger–Spiced Vodka, 274
    Hot Mead, 279
    infused, 271
    Juniper Vodka, 277
    Orange-Rosemary Vodka, 275
    Spicy Lithuanian Vodka, 276

W

Wątróbka w maderze, 174–75
Weeknight Roast Chicken, 156–57
White Barszcz, 78–79
Wiener Schnitzel, Polish Style, 188–89
Wild Mushrooms and Sauerkraut Filling for Pierogi, 210
Winter Roasted Beet Salad, 110
Wiśniówka, 272
Wlosczyzny, 82
Włoska kapusta w białym winie, 118

Z

Zakwas, 78, 79
Ziemniaki z selerem, 123
Zimowa surówka z burakami, 110
Zrazy i kasza grzyczana, 169–70
Zucchini, Garlicky Carrots and, 111
Zupa grzybowa, 69–73
Zupa musztardowa, 88–89
Zupa pomidorowa, 87
Zupa szczawiowa, 75–76
Żurek, 78–79